Don't Believe It For A Minute!

Forty Toxic Ideas
that are
Driving You Crazy

ARNOLD A. LAZARUS, PH.D.

CLIFFORD N. LAZARUS, PH.D.

ALLEN FAY, M.D.

Impact  *Publishers*®
San Luis Obispo, California 93406

Copyright © 1993
by Arnold A. Lazarus
Clifford N. Lazarus
Allen Fay

Library of Congress Cataloging in Publication Data

Lazarus, Arnold A.
   Don't believe it for a minute! : forty toxic ideas
that are driving you crazy / Arnold A. Lazarus, Clifford
N. Lazarus, Allen Fay.
     p.   cm.
   ISBN 0-915166-80-1 (pbk. : alk. paper) :
   1. Conduct of life. 2. Maxims—Psychological aspects.
3. Attitude change. I. Lazarus, Clifford N., 1961- .
II. Fay, Allen.   III. Title.
 BF637.C5L393   1993
 158—dc20   93-4934
                                                 CIP

Printed in the United States of America on acid-free paper
Published by **_Impact_ 🌀 _Publishers_®**
P.O. Box 1094, San Luis Obispo, CA 93406

Toxic Ideas

Acknowledgements

We are extremely grateful to Dr. Albert Ellis, the founder of Rational-Emotive Therapy. We have learned an enormous amount from his numerous publications, workshops and seminars, and from many personal and professional interactions over the years. He knows more about recognizing and conquering toxic misbeliefs than anyone else we have met.

Our thanks also go to two colleagues from London England, Professor Windy Dryden and Dr. Roy Eskapa who offered helpful suggestions and discussed how they apply various "antidotes" when treating their own clients.

Laura Haney perused the initial draft of our manuscript and offered many helpful suggestions.

Our publisher, psychologist Dr. Robert E. Alberti, recommended that we not only examine and refute the toxic misbeliefs, but that we also add specific and positive counter-beliefs. His contributions to style and substance have improved the book immeasurably. We're also much indebted to Stephanie Strickmeier for a thorough copy-edit, bringing clarity and consistency to the work, and helping us translate psychological concepts into everyday language.

Introduction

On Mothers' Day, 1993, a feature article in the *Los Angeles Times* reported on advice from moms — as remembered by their now-adult children. Among the collected wisdom:

Never eat anything bigger than your head.

Keep your mouth shut and your legs crossed.

Never marry a musician.

Those and other bits of folklore, so we're told, have been handed down from mother to child for generations.

That doesn't make them true!

It's amazing how many bright and forward-thinking people, individuals who see themselves as well-informed and enlightened, nevertheless subscribe to ideas and philosophies that subvert their own happiness and undermine the well-being of their friends and families. It is for people who sabotage themselves and those they care about that this book is written.

If you start out on a trip with the wrong directions, chances are you'll get lost. And so it is with the journey through life. There is so much nonsense and misinformation around that most of us have acquired faulty "road maps." As a result, we're diverted into paths that lead nowhere. All too often, we get stuck in patterns that create tension, depression, anxiety, guilt, and anguish.

What are these mistaken ideas, the main toxic misbeliefs that create psychological suffering? What notions and doctrines prevent us from achieving a loving and winning outlook? The forty toxic ideas discussed in this book are the ones we have found most prevalent among our patients. The people who subscribed to these misbeliefs tended to suffer needlessly from emotional misery and displayed widespread psychological difficulties.

It's interesting to note what a wide array of human problems rest on the same underlying errors. General unhappiness, severe stress, chronic frustration, fears and phobias, difficulties relating to other people, a lack of self-confidence, a negative self-concept, and needless guilt are some of the more common consequences.

If you subscribe to many (or any) of these toxic misbeliefs, we invite you to consider carefully the ideas in this book for systematically rethinking and eliminating each of these venomous notions. You're likely to be a lot happier, better able to cope, and less troubled if you do. We believe our straightforward discussion of the toxic misbeliefs and their specific antidotes will prove helpful to you.

You'll undoubtedly notice that many of the Toxic Ideas overlap one another, and that the same themes are often repeated. This is intentional. "Over-learning" through repetition enhances the usefulness of the material, enabling you to remember, retain, and apply it. Please note also that, although some points may seem identical, there are actually subtle but significant differences that need to be appreciated.

Some Toxic Ideas may appear to contradict one another. Thus, Toxic Idea #6 advises you not to walk on eggshells, and to be forthright and open, whereas Toxic Idea #10 points out that total honesty can be destructive and is generally ill-advised. Similarly Toxic Idea #8 strongly advises you to do your loved ones' bidding when feasible, but Toxic Idea #23 emphasizes how important it is to attend to your own needs. Nevertheless, a careful study of the points being emphasized will reveal distinctive differences. It is hoped that the reader will appreciate that what appears to be contradictory is actually complementary.

Some of the misbeliefs are not entirely erroneous — partial truths or half-truths are often what make them dangerous.

Misbeliefs abound. This book is concerned only with those notions that cause emotional suffering and psychological disturbance. We do not discuss many dangerous myths (e.g., "Lightning never strikes in the same place twice,") or simple fallacies (e.g., "Fat people are usually jolly,").

Blatant and very obvious misbeliefs have been excluded also (e.g., "Because my father smoked and drank and lived to be 86, there's no need for me to quit smoking or watch my drinking," or "If you want to get ahead, make sure that you bully and intimidate your subordinates"). The vast majority of people realize that beliefs of that sort are destructive and false. Rather, the misbeliefs included in this book are ones that the three of us hear virtually every day in our consulting rooms. Even some highly intelligent and well-educated people have been duped into believing them. And by believing them, they often have suffered considerable and entirely unnecessary emotional, psychological, and social problems.

Although we encounter patients who express sexist, racist and other bigoted sentiments, these social issues are frequently addressed elsewhere; we have not included them here. Bigotry and prejudice are important sources of emotional pain, of course, reflecting fear, ignorance and toxic early learning. They demand methods of correction beyond the scope of this book.

People in need of psychotherapy often display all-or-nothing thinking, over-generalization, labeling and mislabeling, exaggeration and magnification of problems, and other so-called "cognitive distortions." If challenged, few believers will actually defend these positions. However, many are not aware of their faulty thinking and some cannot see or will not admit that it is faulty, even when it is pointed out to them. Nevertheless, if you inquire: "Do you really believe that things are either good or bad, black or white, right or wrong, and that there are no exceptions, middle-of-the-road, or gray areas?" most people will acknowledge that things fall on a continuum, and they admit to the mistake of thinking in absolutistic ways. By contrast, those who subscribe to certain toxic misbeliefs outlined herein will defend their veracity.

Thus, take Toxic Idea #1, RECREATION IS A WASTE OF TIME. Those who are committed to the notion that the sole purpose of life is to have an impact, to leave a mark, to make a lasting impression, are unlikely to be persuaded by our reasoning. Nor are harsh disciplinarians likely to abandon their punitive ways after reading Toxic Idea #15, PUNISHMENT IS GOOD DISCIPLINE. And timid people-pleasers will probably not be inclined to abandon their self-defeating tendencies after reading Toxic Idea #6, DON'T SAY THINGS THAT MIGHT HURT OTHERS' FEELINGS, or Toxic Idea #23, DON'T BE SELFISH; PUT OTHERS FIRST. But we hope to reach those readers whose toxic misbeliefs are not deeply entrenched so that they are amenable to simple logic and careful rethinking.

By reading and applying the material in this book you almost surely will be able to identify one, two, several, or many toxic misbeliefs that cause you to suffer needless unhappiness and dissatisfaction. But more importantly, by implementing the various antidotes presented, you will be able to "detoxify" your thinking, thus paving the way for a more balanced, psychologically healthy and satisfying life.

We follow the same format in each instance. For each Toxic Idea, we provide an *Example,* followed by an *Analysis, Antidotes* in the form of self-statements that counter the misbelief, and finally end the section with a *Positive Counter-Belief.* We believe that this straightforward format makes the book easy to read, easy to understand, easy to remember, and easy for interested readers to apply the corrective recommendations as needed.

Psychologically uneven people, who are well-rehearsed toxic thinkers, cannot realistically expect to correct their lack of mental balance by merely repeating a few positive thoughts once in a while. Rather, such individuals, in order to override their well-developed "negative self-talk," will at first want to practice strengthening their "straight-thinking." This means that in addition to reading and repeating the positive self-statements and corrective counter-beliefs in this book, it is important to rehearse them actively and consistently several times a day.

One good rule of thumb: every time you catch yourself thinking a toxic or negative thought, make yourself consider at least two (more is better) positive self-statements or healthy counter-beliefs. This will help you work toward increasing psychological balance. At first this mental exercise might seem unnatural, but after a little practice, you will feel an increasing sense of familiarity with positive thoughts, making it progressively easier to achieve a more balanced mind and and a winning and loving lifestyle.

How Many Toxic Ideas Do You Hold?

Now it's time for you to take a look at your own toxic misbeliefs. By answering the following brief questionnaire and then heeding the instructions right after it, you'll learn more about your own faulty thinking, and will derive the maximum benefit from this book.

Beliefs Questionnaire

Listed below are 40 statements. Read each one carefully and decide whether you basically agree or disagree with it. Place a check mark alongside those beliefs with which you tend to agree. Keep in mind that there are no absolutely right or wrong answers.

1 _____ Recreation is a waste of time
2 _____ You're better off when you control other people
3 _____ It's healthy to "blow off steam"

4 _____ Family and friends should love you no matter how you act

5 _____ Kindness will overcome unkindness

6 _____ Don't say things that might hurt others' feelings

7 _____ Perfection should be your goal

8 _____ Say "No" — If you give 'em an inch, they'll take a mile

9 _____ Ultimatums settle disputes

10 _____ Total honesty is the best policy

11 _____ Inconsiderate relatives or friends deserve the silent treatment

12 _____ You can achieve almost anything

13 _____ If you want something done right, do it yourself

14 _____ When things go wrong, find someone to blame

15 _____ Punishment is good discipline

16 _____ Keep your feelings to yourself

17 _____ First impressions tell you what people are really like

18 _____ Your parents' approval is most important

19 _____ Success and money lead to happiness

20 _____ Once a victim, always a victim

21 _____ Be modest; don't flatter yourself

22 _____ Criticism is a good way to correct people's mistakes

23 _____ Don't be selfish; put others first

24 _____ Your spouse should love your parents and family

25 _____ We all do our best when we have high expectations

26 _____ It's important to be liked by everyone

27 _____ Problems disappear if you ignore them

28 _____ If you play, play to win

29 _____ Have definite rules for yourself and others

30 _____ Anyone who truly loves you should know what you need

31 _____ Insults are bound to be upsetting

32 _____ Being hard on yourself is good for you

33 _____ An apology wipes the slate clean

34 _____ To change you must understand the reasons for your behavior

35 _____ Cover your mistakes; the important thing is to be right

36 _____ You won't go wrong if you follow your gut feelings

37 _____ Life should be fair

38 _____ Happily married people don't have sexual feelings for anyone else

39 _____ Your word is your bond; never break a promise

40 _____ Suffering and hard work build character

We regard each of these 40 beliefs as false and potentially toxic. As you read *Don't Believe It for a Minute!* pay special attention to the arguments presented against those that you have checked off — which you apparently regard as valid or correct. Does our reasoning lead you to rethink or reconsider your position? We certainly hope so. Some of the toxic misbeliefs are more injurious than others, but we maintain that all can have damaging and destructive consequences. Although you may find some examples rather extreme (they are usually drawn from the cases of people who were very unhappy or disturbed), please understand that *any* degree of faulty reasoning (crooked thinking) can have far-reaching negative consequences. Good feelings (emotional balance) and effective living depend largely on clear (rational, logical, accurate) thinking. *As you think, so shall you feel and act.*

We think you'll find it valuable to examine your own ideas about how life is supposed to work, and to reconsider those that may be driving *you* crazy. You *can* change your attitudes and, when it comes to be toxic misbeliefs in this book, we encourage you to do so. In fact, we urge you — in the name of good mental health — to follow this simple advice: consider each toxic idea carefully, then *Don't Believe It for a Minute!*

Toxic Idea #1

Recreation Is A Waste Of Time

Harry, a 50-year-old professor, was accustomed to working 100 or more hours per week. For him, social gatherings, plays, movies, concerts, vacations, games and other recreational activities were a waste of time. "Instead of frittering away my valuable time," he said, "I could be reading a journal, writing a paper, performing an experiment, or doing something else worthwhile." The only relaxation he allowed himself was reading the newspaper. Nobody, including Harry himself, would call him a happy person or would say that he enjoyed life. In addition, despite the amount of time and effort he expended on his work, Harry received little recognition, and was often passed over for promotion.

Analysis

While only a few share Harry's extreme views, many people are overwhelmed, stressed out and exhausted because they take on more work than they can handle and because they think they can accomplish a great deal by "working around the clock." These folks believe that the purpose of life is to work hard, achieve, win, get ahead, compete, and succeed at almost any cost. They view themselves as productive, and they often gain the tangible rewards of high productivity — usually money and what it can buy.

Some "productive" people go even further, however: like Harry, they regard idleness as sinful and equate almost any form of pure fun and recreation with a lazy, indolent, slothful, shiftless existence. To them, recreation, does not seem fruitful; its intangible rewards — fun, enjoyment, relaxation — are not proof of hard work. These people underestimate the productive impact proper recreation can provide, and they fail to take enough breaks during the workday to keep themselves alert and focused.

In addition to believing that recreation is unproductive, many people also believe it diverts their attention from the ultimate goal of their work: acquiring financial security and career status. Of course, saving a lot of money for the "golden years" of retirement makes sense. But there may be problems with such postponed gratification. Some people die before they retire, and others become too ill to enjoy the fruits of their labors. Still others despite many years of hard work, may have amassed fewer assets than anticipated. Moreover, many retirees do not fully enjoy life because they don't know how! Workaholics all their lives, they have not developed leisure pursuits or recreational activities and find themselves without interests or passions worth pursuing.

Because both work and play are essential for healthy living, you need to aim for balance. If you genuinely enjoy hard work, go to it. But make sure that you "waste" enough time in order to revitalize yourself, to prevent burnout and stress. To "goof off" now and then will tend to keep you fresh and alert and enable you to do justice to whatever tasks are really essential. "I love taking long walks, especially in the country," one of our patients said, "but whenever I take walks, I feel guilty because I have so many important things do." But those long walks are likely to keep him healthy and able to do "important things" for many years to come. By engaging in pleasurable activities without guilt and by realizing that mixing fun with work will lead to greater productivity in the long run, he will also enhance the quality of his life.

Many psychological studies have shown that "distributed practice" (e.g., leisure activities interspersed with your work) actually enhances the quality and productivity of your output. Fun and games "recharge your batteries," and enable you to concentrate better and work more effectively. Only a few individuals can sustain concentrated attention for more than a couple of hours without needing to take a 10-15 minute break. In fact, a person who sticks to a task for a solid eight hours will usually accomplish far less than someone who takes ten-minute breaks every hour or so (and thus puts in fewer than seven hours of effort).

Continuous work without rest undermines your efficiency. When you pause for rest, it's important to involve yourself in an activity that differs from the task at hand. Thus, if you're doing paperwork or reading academic material, turning to the newspaper or even comic books for relaxation will tend to be less refreshing than a non-reading change of pace, such as a brisk walk or calling a friend.

Remember you may work more and accomplish less unless you incorporate recreation into your daily life.

Antidotes

Corrective Self-Statements

> *"People need down-time to recharge their batteries."*

> *"I deserve to have fun in my life."*

> *"All work and no play are not good for anybody."*

> *"More work may mean less output."*

> *"It's better to work to live than to live to work."*

> *"I'll be more productive if I have fun in my life."*

> *"Time enjoyed is never wasted."*

> *"If I don't enjoy myself now, it may be too late in the future."*

Positive Counter-Belief

> *Rest, fun and relaxation*
> *are important basic needs.*

Toxic Idea #2

You're Better Off When You Control Other People

Even as a child, Kay was called "bossy." She knew she wasn't "popular," but never realized how uncomfortable most people were with her controlling ways. When she married, she chose a rather passive man whom she kept under her thumb with such injunctions as, "Be home by six." "Stop spending so much time with your sister." "Get off the phone." "Mow the grass instead of watching TV." Within two years, Tom left her. Kay's first reaction was typical of her: she told all their acquaintances to choose between her and her husband. "If I hear that you've had anything to do with Tom, I don't want to see you again."

Analysis

Nobody likes to be told what to do. Little wonder that Kay had such trouble maintaining relationships. Spouses who try to boss their partners around inevitably arouse hostility and resentment. Dictatorial employers lose good employees, and those who stay find ways to sabotage the dictator. People who try to control their friends usually make enemies.

We often see couples like Kay and Tom in our psychotherapy practices. One partner tries to keep a tight rein on the other, and neither person is apt to be happy.

Everyone is an individual and has the right to live life according to his or her own "script" (although it certainly makes sense to prevent someone from doing something that would clearly harm him/herself or others). "Live and let live" — the old cliché that suggests we interfere with others as little as possible — is a policy that usually pays handsome emotional dividends.

People like Kay, who don't mind their own business, who frequently tell others what to do, and who need to control others, are often anxious and insecure themselves. Those who try to stand in the way of other people's wishes usually fail to gain the control they seek — and they fail to hold on to friends.

If you want to get along with people, if you would like to be regarded as lovable and decent, it pays to give up attempts to control them. You may want to ask yourself: Do I tend to be controlling? Be honest. Do you like to give free advice? Do you frequently tell others what and what not to do? Do you usually try to get your own way? Do you enjoy giving commands and issuing instructions? When you are annoyed with someone, do you sulk or pout? Do you ever make threats? Do you try to "get even?" If you answered "yes" to any of these questions, chances are that a lot of people resent you.

If someone else's actions will seriously inconvenience you, or if someone is trying to control you, and you want to do something about it, you're more likely to gain cooperation and consideration by simply *asking* him or her not to do it, rather than by making threats or demands. If your attempts to remedy the situation fail, our advice is to distance yourself from that person. This includes anyone and everyone, even parents, siblings, other family members, employers, and anybody you consider a friend.

Of course, there are situations where it is necessary for people to know who's the boss, who's in charge. Emergencies demand strong leadership, and employment situations generally require supervisors. In most walks of life, however, equality and mutual respect prove more rewarding, particularly in intimate relationships.

We've all had more than enough controls imposed on us: parental injunctions, school rules, job policies, government regulations. If you try to keep someone "under your thumb," chances are that person will find a way of rebelling. You, and everyone with whom you associate are better off when you're non-demanding and non-controlling.

Express yourself assertively when the situation requires it. Otherwise, as they say in the advice columns, MYOB.

Antidotes
Corrective Self-Statements
Repeat to yourself:
"It's better to request rather than to demand."

"Live and let live."

"Nobody likes to be told how to live or what to do."

"We all have to accept certain things even if we don't like them."

"It's better to cooperate than to control."

"People are entitled to write their own scripts."

"I can't legislate how others should act."

Positive Counter-Belief

You'll get along better if you don't try to control others.

It's Healthy To "Blow Off Steam"

Melvin was inclined to "fly off the handle." His temper cost him several jobs, two marriages that ended in acrimonious divorces, and many friendships. "I don't care about that," he said. "I'm not about to keep my feelings in and to sit on my emotions. My sister's like that and she has migraine headaches. I'd rather be healthy, alive and friendless than blow a gasket, die, and have a big funeral where people would say what a sweet guy I was."

Analysis

Melvin, like many people, believes that if he doesn't blow off steam when he's angry, the forces and pressures of the emotions dammed up inside him can literally cause his blood vessels to explode. Thus, Melvin thinks that "flying off the handle" is a healthy way to express his anger.

Denying or suppressing your feelings, perhaps doing little more than smiling sweetly when you're angry or annoyed, is unhealthy. In fact, most experts would advise you to *express* anger, not suppress it. It is better to "get it out."

But how are these feelings best expressed? Do you think you need to raise your voice, pound your desk, shake your fists, and stomp your feet? If you're angry, should you really tell people off? Will yelling and screaming give you the upper hand? The answer to all of these questions is a resounding "No"! Many people who explode the way Melvin does tend to be seen as aggressive. They don't know how to express their feelings calmly. Blowing up, involving a loss of control, may lead to a temporary feeling of satisfaction and relief at having "beaten" someone. But afterwards, many people remain just as upset as before the "explosion," and others feel frightened after losing control.

People who act assertively, however, deal with minor annoyances before they become major confrontations; they resist unreasonable demands; they ask for what they want; they take a stand without venting their rage or putting down other people. In other words, they express their anger and other strong emotions firmly, directly, and rationally.

Direct statements are far more effective than emotional tirades. Here's an example: In the following exchanges between "Dennis" and "Jack," imagine you are

Dennis. How would you respond to Jack's tirade and to his direct statement? Here is Jack's angry blast at Dennis: "You bastard! Who the hell do you think you are? How dare you go over my head and talk to my boss about your workload?" Jack's direct statement to Dennis: "I am angry that you went over my head and spoke to my boss about your workload. If we are going to get along together, you'd better not do this sort of thing in the future." Jack's direct statement expresses the anger without repression or denial, and Dennis' response is more likely to be positive. Responding assertively, not only are you apt to get better results, but you'll also be less likely to damage your own health.

Antidotes

Corrective Self-Statements

> *"Anger is okay, but is best expressed assertively, not aggressively."*

> *"Losing your cool puts you at a disadvantage."*

> *"If the tables were turned, how would I want anger expressed to me?"*

> *"Other people and things have too much power over me if I can become so enraged."*

> *"Only my own thinking can make me mad."*

Positive Counter-Belief

"Blowing off steam" is self-defeating; it's healthy to express emotions assertively.

Family And Friends Should Love You No Matter How You Act

Millie, a 65-year-old widow, has three adult children who live within commuting distance, but she complains bitterly that they rarely call and hardly ever visit her. She is extremely critical and virtually nobody wants her company. She has picked on her children throughout their lives, and even now, as adults, the limited contact they have with their mother is filled with fault-finding, reprimands, and rebukes. No wonder they keep away. "They should love and respect me because I am their mother," Millie wails.

Analysis

Some people, like Millie, believe in "unconditional love." No matter how obnoxiously they may act, their closest relatives and true friends should continue to love them for "themselves." This is a mistaken notion. Unconditional love is possible between parents and young children, but in most relationships, your conduct will determine who loves you, hates you, seeks you out, or avoids you. After all, others use the track record of your actions — which speak louder than words — to form opinions about you. You know your own inner thoughts and motives, but the only information other people have to go on is how you *act*, which is up to you.

People respond to what you *do* to and for them, regardless of who and what you *are*. Susie, a newlywed, complained that her husband, Ron, had developed the habit of visiting his sister on the way home from work or stopping off at the local pub for a beer with the boys. Susie explained, "I'm his wife, and he should want to be with me instead of choosing to be with his sister or his friends." Ron, however, had reasons for taking his time on the way home: The moment he walked through the door, Susie would assail him with a list of chores and complaints.

Take a hard, honest look at your actions and ask what you do to and for the important people in your life. First, ask yourself if your personality and style make you lovable and ensure that your company is worth seeking. Do you have a pleasant disposition? Are you easy to get along with? Are you helpful and obliging? Do you express affection? Do you show concern? Are you a good listener?

Then ask yourself if you, like Millie, treat others badly. Are you petty, nasty, rude, or sullen? Are you generally critical? Do you often express disapproval? Do you often complain, make accusations, fly off the handle? Do you simply not pay attention to others? Even when you perform good deeds, do you do so reluctantly or unpleasantly? If you often respond negatively to those closest to you, they, like Millie's children, will tend to distance themselves from you — even if they do love and respect you.

Nobody can be sweet, warm, kind, loving, considerate, caring, and pleasant 100% of the time. The question to ask yourself is how often and under what circumstances you're selfish or uncaring. Remember, you reveal your love through your actions! If you discover inconsistencies between who you are and how you act, you'll want to change your actions. For example, if you view yourself as generous, but manage never to pick up the check, better make it a point to *ask* the waiter to give it to you. If you admire a colleague's work, *say* so. If you consider punctuality important, don't keep others waiting.

John discovered why such a change can be necessary: "I'm Claire's husband, so she should love me because that's what wives are supposed to do. But when, with her help, I realized that I am often unpleasant and picky, I began to change my attitude and my ways. Instead of criticizing the housekeeping, I pitched in because I realized it's my house too. After all, she's balancing her business career with her career as wife and mother."

Antidotes

Corrective Self-Statements

> *"People can't read my mind, but they can see my actions."*

> *"Our actions define us as individuals."*

> *"If I want people to treat me nicely, I need to act pleasantly toward them."*

Positive Counter-Belief

How you act is more important than who you are.

Kindness Will Overcome Unkindness

Sally's husband was often abusive. One morning, over breakfast, Hugh began to shout at her because she was on the phone instead of keeping him company. Later that morning, she picked up his shirts from the laundry, ran some other errands for him, and decided to cook his favorite dish for dinner. They had agreed from the beginning of their marriage that Hugh would work for pay and Sally would keep their home, and she thought that if she could only create an "ideal" loving home atmosphere, his abusive behavior would stop.

Analysis

Sally was rewarding her husband's negative behavior. In response to his outbursts, Hugh found his chores done for him and he was served his favorite dinner. Why would he change his treatment of his wife when she responds so positively? Behavior is influenced largely by its consequences. The events that follow an action will weaken or strengthen it. If Sally is nice to Hugh when he treats her badly, she is *teaching him* to continue being abusive. If she showed him instead that she was willing to be especially kind and helpful only when he was considerate and loving, a positive pattern might be more likely to develop.

Spousal abuse is a complex problem, of course, and Hugh didn't *start* abusing Sally because she was nice to him. Chances are he himself was abused as a child (most abusers have been victims). The problem here, however, is that Sally has let Hugh know that *it's okay* for him to abuse her; she'll even do special favors for him in spite of his being abusive. To a large degree, *we teach others how to treat us.* By enduring — and even rewarding — Hugh's abusive behavior, Sally gives him the message that it's okay to treat her that way. It's time for her to interrupt that downward cycle.

Corwin was one of our patients who believed this toxic idea. He would send flowers to his wife whenever she flared up at him. He hoped this gesture would put her in a good mood. Instead, it simply encouraged her to flare up at him even more. Do not reinforce behaviors in others that you wish to eliminate.

Your goal should be to discourage offensive behavior from anyone.

Often, we see people who seem trapped in untenable work situations, in which employers or supervisors treat them poorly, and they are afraid to speak up. In many instances, the mistreatment is too high a price to pay for job security. If you're in such a situation and you cannot rectify matters, you may be better off seeking other employment. This is tough advice to take when jobs are hard to come by, but if the situation is out of hand, you must make the choice to care for yourself. (Fortunately, anti-harrassment laws afford some protection to employees these days. That may make the choice a bit easier.)

Some of the most unhappy instances involve women who are, like Sally, trapped in abusive marriages. Many endure callous treatment and stay married because of religious beliefs or financial constraints. No matter how much love and kindness they show their husbands, these women see no end to the sadistic experiences. (When confronted by domestic physical violence in our practices, we often involve the police, other social agencies, and/or relatives with the power to end such behaviors. No one deserves to be abused.)

We applaud kindness in relationships, but not in response to abuse. Actor Alan Alda said it well: "Be fair with others, but then keep after them until they're fair with you."

Antidotes
Corrective Self-Statements
> *"I do not have to take abuse from anyone."*

> *"I must learn to speak up if I don't like the way I am being treated."*

"I will not reward unkind behavior from others."

"It's okay to request courteous and fair treatment from everyone."

"If someone treats me badly I will not smile and pretend it's okay."

Positive Counter-Belief

Unkindness deserves a firm response;
don't let anyone abuse you.

Toxic Idea #6

Don't Say Things That Might Hurt Others' Feelings

Billy was described as a person with "an attitude problem" at work. He was often rude to customers, irritable with his subordinates, and too pushy at sales meetings. Behind his back, people often commented about his behavior, but nobody said anything to Billy because they "didn't want to hurt his feelings." Underneath it all, he was perceived as a nice-enough guy. If someone had cared to take the risk of offending him, he might have had a chance to shape up. But nobody wanted to risk hurting his feelings by pointing out his poor style. Eventually, Billy's offensive manner cost him his job.

Analysis

Strictly speaking, it is impossible to "hurt someone's feelings." We may allow others' words to hurt us, but we don't have to get upset by what others say, no matter how much we dislike it. But few individuals are truly frank and forthright. Often, people wallow in their misery simply because nobody cares enough, or has the guts to set them straight. Television commercials often suggest an indirect mode of giving feedback — leave dandruff shampoos and mouthwashes in conspicuous places, hoping that the offenders will catch on, wise up, get the message. Doesn't it make more sense to discuss such matters with people directly, but tactfully?

If people get upset at things they would rather not hear, they'll get over it and at least have a chance to make constructive changes. Remember that you can hurt people with sticks and stones, but they hurt themselves with your words. The age-old saying, "Sometimes we have to be cruel in order to be kind" is profoundly true. There is a world of difference between trying to annihilate someone via deliberate and vicious attacks, by searching for the most devastating putdowns and criticisms imaginable, and by tactfully drawing attention to events, facts, or situations that they can remedy.

Bert squeezed himself into his old dinner jacket and asked his wife how he looked. "Either lose weight or have it altered," she said curtly. Bert, who had gained 20 lbs., allowed his feelings to get hurt over her remark. Perhaps he wanted her to lie, but what good would that have done? We're not recommending a tactless or thoughtless assault in the guise of helpfulness. The way you say something is extremely important. You can be tactful, diplomatic, discreet and appropriately honest at the same time. Thus, Bert's wife could simply have said: "It looks a bit snug to me, honey," and let it go at that.

One of our colleagues wondered why two of his associates never asked him to join them for lunch. We told him straight out, "They don't like your table manners, especially the fact that you chew with your mouth open." He promptly mended his ways and was no longer excluded.

One method of tactful criticism involves the "sandwich technique" wherein you precede any negative feedback with a positive remark and then end on an equally positive note. Don't make your critique a direct attack: "This chicken is tough and too salty; you really need to learn how to cook!" Try this instead: "I can see you really put a lot of effort into this meal. I prefer chicken a bit less salty, but the sweet potatoes and the appetizers were delicious."

Antidotes

Corrective Self-Statements

> *"What you say is often less important than how you say it."*

> *"If I think it's important I will speak my mind, even if others object."*

> *"It's okay to give honest feedback or input as long as it is constructively intended."*

> *"It is sometimes necessary to be a little hurtful in order to be helpful."*

> *"It is usually better to be direct and outspoken than to drop subtle hints."*

Positive Counter-Belief

If it's important, say it, but be tactful.

Toxic Idea #7

Perfection Should Be Your Goal

Henry worked very hard and tried to prove to his bosses that his work was perfect. In fact, his priorities were such that his job came before anyone and everything. It cost him two marriages, but still he believed in giving 100% at the office. He received several promotions and bonuses at work, but in spite of his devotion, he was one of the first to be laid off when his company decided to retrench. Coworkers were uncomfortable in his presence, and some supervisors felt threatened by him. Moreover, his failure to relax over the years and ease up at times seemed to have caused physical problems which his doctors attributed to stress.

Analysis

Henry and many people like him who strive to give 100 percent all the time are being unrealistic. They're demanding perfection from themselves, not realizing that few things and no people are perfect. Expecting perfection — measuring yourself against this impossible standard — can result in a downward spiral of negative thinking that can often lead to dissatisfaction, self-criticism, resentment, and a "why bother" attitude. If you push yourself to perform perfectly the way Henry does, you may find that your efforts are counterproductive. Forcing yourself to meet unrealistic expectations invites undue stress, anxiety, absenteeism, and burnout. In fact, perfectionism often encourages unhealthy competition and may even promote unethical behavior (cheating on exams, taking credit for others' work, falsely claiming job qualifications).

After admitting how unrealistic your standard of perfection is, learn to give yourself permission not to perform at optimum speed every minute of the day. Instead, strive to be competent, to do your best work, realizing that there are days when you feel ill, you are preoccupied with a personal problem, or you find that the task at hand just does not seem important. Freed from the pressure to perform perfectly, you will enjoy the work more, and the result will be good, maybe excellent, work anyway. In fact, you will often experience a great deal of satisfaction from work that turns out less than perfect. For example, after Arthur had spent two weeks painting his den, the job was far from perfect, but certainly more than adequate. Besides, Arthur thoroughly enjoyed the process and the outcome. Henry could learn a valuable lesson from Arthur about the difference between the frustration of striving for perfection and the satisfaction of achieving excellence.

Henry also needs to learn how to make time for relaxation — leisure, fun, and games — outside of the workday to enhance his efficiency and performance at work.

(Related Toxic Idea: #1 "RECREATION IS A WASTE OF TIME.")

Antidotes

Corrective Self-Statements

> *"Perfectionism usually leads to frustration and disappointment."*

> *"Some things only need to be good enough."*

> *"If you aim too high, you will miss the mark."*

> *"The outcome is often less important than the enjoyment derived from doing the task."*

> *"I do not always have to do my best."*

Positive Counter-Belief

> *Aim for excellence*
> *rather than perfection.*

Toxic Idea #8

Say "No" — If You Give 'em An Inch, They'll Take A Mile

Whenever Lisa's children asked permission to do something, the invariable answer was "no." When her husband requested a favor of her, she often refused. At work, she was disliked by almost everyone because of her automatic "no." She did not realize how dearly she was paying for this attitude. She sensed that virtually nobody was truly fond of her. She came for therapy after her husband threatened to divorce her.

Analysis

Assertive people know how to refuse unreasonable requests, how to say "no" to excessive demands from others, and how to stand up for their rights. Indeed, when a pesky salesperson comes on strong, the ability to say "no" is a useful skill, but when dealing with loved ones, the consequences are very different. With intimates, it is disruptive to say "no" unless you have a very good reason.

Parents are often the worst offenders, saying "no" to their children when it would have been to everyone's advantage to have said "yes," or at least to have had a dialogue with the child. For example, 16-year-old Pam was eager to see a school football game in which her boyfriend was to be the quarterback. The game was scheduled to start at 5 p.m. Her father refused to let Pam go because he wanted the whole family at the dinner table before six o'clock. In the end the girl stormed out of the house, missed eating dinner, upset the entire family, and was miserable and unhappy herself. How much better if her father had realized how important the game was to Pam and had not stood in her way.

We have seen many distressed families, like Lisa's, where the major problem hinged around a "no"-sayer, a parent who thought that it was good upbringing to allow very few privileges and rarely grant favors. Saying "no" without a truly valid reason only breeds resentment. Arbitrary no-saying usually comes across as rejection. This does not imply that you have to do everything your loved ones want you to do. If you have a valid reason for declining to do something, simply state it.

Why not be accommodating in intimate relationships? What's wrong with doing everything possible to say "yes"?

If a loved one says, "Will you do me a favor," try to respond with, "Sure, what is it?" Saying, "No" will breed anything but love, caring and closeness. Asking, "What is it?" is not as bad, but the best answer is an affirmative one. If the request is unreasonable or inconvenient, one can renegotiate. "I'd be glad to pick up your laundry and take Sean to soccer practice, but unfortunately I don't get out of work today before seven."

Are there no limits? Must you do anything a family member asks of you? Of course that's not what we mean to suggest. You need to protect the integrity of your own time and needs. And your family must learn that they can't "take a mile" by expecting you *always* to accommodate their every whim. What's important here is *balance*. You don't have to give them everything they ask for, but you should say "no" to the *automatic* "no" in yourself. Some of their requests may be very rewarding for *you*: "Hey dad, let's play catch!" "Mom, can you come to school for the class play?" "Honey, if you'll pick up the car from the garage, I'll take you to lunch at the wharf."

In short, look for reasons to say "yes" to your loved ones. Saying "no" too often may just slam the door of happiness in your face.

Antidotes
Corrective Self-Statements

> *"It is good to refuse unreasonable requests, but it is foolish to say 'no' without good reason."*

"If I say 'no,' it's best to explain my reasons clearly."

"Relationships benefit more from consent and approval than from forbiddance and refusal."

"Refusing to grant a favor is often perceived as a form of rejection."

Positive Counter-Belief

If you value a relationship, say "yes" whenever you can.

Ultimatums Settle Disputes

Fred thought it was smart to lay down the law. One of his favorite lines was, "It's either my way or the highway." He was not well-liked. During heated negotiations at work, he would often say, "Get back to me by 4 p.m. tomorrow or the deal's off." He won some victories through intimidation, but he sustained greater losses. His biggest loss came when his fiancée broke off their engagement because he had issued an ultimatum during a minor disagreement. Fred objected when she wished to spend the weekend with her favorite aunt who was visiting from abroad. "Make a choice," he said. "You either spend Saturday and Sunday with me or we forget about getting married." His fiancée gave back the ring and refused to have anything more to do with him.

Analysis

Coercion, threats, browbeating, and ultimatums may be useful between enemies in a state of war: "You have until daybreak to remove your troops or we will call in our air force!" An ultimatum is essentially a "do-this-or-else" communication. It employs pressure, threat, coercion, and intimidation, tactics necessary in war. An ultimatum shuts down communication. In fact, it is the opposite of compromise, negotiation, empathy and understanding — the components of any wholesome exchange. It's a power play that doesn't belong in any relationship in which respect, consideration, caring, or love are significant elements. People who use ultimatums in interpersonal relationships are displaying ignorance or weakness.

Such strong-arm tactics, then, have no place either at work or at home. Employers who issue ultimatums usually end up being hated, and any cooperation they receive is likely to be temporary and superficial. Decreased production and even sabotage are likely. For example, one of our patients confided: "When my boss said I had to have a project on his desk by 2:00 'or else!', I was so mad that I made up my mind to thwart him. So at 1:30 I pretended to be ill and went home. He didn't get my completed work until the next day, but he couldn't fire me because it wasn't my fault. I was supposedly too ill at the time!"

Intimidation does not breed love and loyalty. In fact, such tactics distance, maybe even alienate, others and cause resentment and bitterness. Thus, it is even more unfortunate when parents and children or spouses use these tactics. Sarah's parents expected her to be home by midnight on weekends without exception. On a recent Saturday night, her car stalled in her boyfriend Hal's driveway just when she needed to leave to meet the 12:00 curfew. After she and Hal tried to jumpstart the car without success, Sarah telephoned to explain the dilemma to her parents and to tell them that Hal's dad would bring her home after having the car towed to the nearest service station. His reaction to her story was to exclaim, "You'll be grounded for a month! You have to be home by midnight or else! No exceptions!"

To repeat: If it has a place, an ultimatum can be issued on a battlefield, in very tough business negotiations, or as a last resort in a confrontation with an unreasonable or bullheaded individual. But to think that this type of behavior has any place in ongoing relationships is like mistaking the neighborhood bully for a trusted friend.

Wise people don't bark commands, issue ultimatums, or tell others what to do. They make requests and share their feelings. To say, in effect, "If you do (or don't do) X, I'll be very hurt," is not usually toxic. If the recipient conveys that he or she couldn't care less about your feelings, there is little point in continuing the discussion (or perhaps the relationship). In any event, issuing an ultimatum won't accomplish your objectives in the long run. You are better off developing a frame of mind in which you are willing to compromise and negotiate. Whenever you use coercion and intimidation, you'll probably lose out in the end. Negotiation and compromise go much farther.

Antidotes

Corrective Self-Statements

> *"An ultimatum is one sure way of hurting a friendship."*

"Threats and ultimatums only shut down communication."

"It's best to express my desires and wishes without ramming them down anyone's throat."

"Even if others obey ultimatums, they usually resent them and will probably try to retaliate."

"People have the right to do as they please, even if I don't like it."

"My own children do not exist to live up to my expectations."

Positive Counter-Belief

Negotiation and compromise settle disputes.

Total Honesty Is The Best Policy

Marvin believed that it was best to be totally and completely "open and honest" with his wife. He disclosed everything about himself, hid no feelings from her, and even shared his innermost fantasies. His frequent unrestrained criticism of her was brutally frank. Indeed, there was something hostile about his compulsive truth-telling. His wife eventually became so upset and turned off by some of Marvin's hurtful disclosures that she divorced him.

Analysis

Marvin believed in unrestrained self-disclosure in the guise of "total honesty." We have seen many patients like Marvin who think that intimate relationships thrive when partners don't censor themselves at all. Complete and absolute openness is the goal. As Marriette told us, "I tell Harold everything; I hide absolutely nothing from him. He knows my most intimate thoughts, feelings, and fantasies, and he is privy to everything I have ever done."

The fault in this toxic idea lies in "total," not in "honesty." Few relationships can tolerate a degree of sharing in which someone withholds virtually nothing and expresses almost everything. Indeed, a simple display of tact and diplomacy often calls for certain things to remain unsaid and for specific truths to be downplayed. For unnecessary, intrusive, unhelpful, and upsetting truth-telling can be deadly. Almost as much pain has been inflicted by indiscriminate truths as by blatant lies. In fact, more often than not, compulsive truth-tellers show no respect for the feelings of others. (However, the blunt, unvarnished truth may prove helpful under the type of circumstances mentioned in Toxic Idea #6 DON'T HURT OTHERS' FEELINGS.)

Marge's therapist advised her to "wipe the slate clean" and tell her husband about the brief affair she had had four years earlier. What dreadful advice! What's done is done. Unfortunately, Marge followed her therapist's recommendation, made her belated confession, and found that it literally tore her marriage apart.

In our practices, examples of sheer boorishness in the guise of honesty are very prevalent. Zak's was a typical case. He often made disparaging comparisons between his wife and other women. Whenever his behavior was questioned, he would reply, "I'm just being honest." Similarly, Howard describes himself as a "straight shooter" who takes pride in "telling it like it is." His job record showed that he was frequently passed over for promotions by people with less talent (but more tact) and that he had been fired from so many jobs that his entire employment future was threatened.

The main point underlying this misbelief is that honesty is indeed a virtue, that without integrity we have no basis for trustworthy communications, and yet anything, even honesty, can be taken too far. The virtues of truth and honor cannot be overstated, but if they are expressed excessively or inappropriately, unfortunate consequences may follow.

Here is a simple test. Ask yourself: Will telling the blunt or naked truth really help? If so, go ahead and pull no punches. If not, let it remain unsaid. Thus, when Yvonne's latest boyfriend with whom she had fallen deeply in love asked how many men she had gone to bed with, she replied with total honesty, "I'm not sure, but there must have been about 60 or 70." She was devastated when he ended the relationship. Perhaps she would have been wiser to have simply said, "Instead of talking about ancient history, let's concentrate on what we have together." She could have added, "By the way, I am not HIV positive and I don't have any other sexually transmitted diseases."

Please understand that the antidote for this toxic idea is *not* "Dishonesty is the best policy." We are only arguing against *total* and *indiscriminate* honesty and stressing that tact and discretion play important roles in our day-to-day interactions. It may seem strange to some that this point needs to be emphasized. But remember that the toxic ideas in this book have come from the people we see in therapy, many of whom subscribe to the notion that *total* honesty is indeed a virtue. We have even heard people argue that tactfulness is a synonym for phoniness and is to be deplored!

Compulsive truth-telling may not be as damaging as compulsive lying, but it can often be devastating. So-called "white lies" are best employed when the truth can only hurt or harm. Thus, when 72-year-old Celia lost her husband after 50 years of marriage and said to her only son, "I was a very good wife. Don't you agree?", he simply answered, "Sure." Privately, he told us that his mother had shown a rather selfish streak throughout her marriage and that she had frequently been short-tempered and over-critical of her husband. But her son would have gained nothing by disagreeing with her assessment by saying, "To be perfectly honest, I think that you were too selfish and critical to consider yourself a very good wife." He told a harmless lie when he said "sure," but he had spared his mother unnecessary hurt.

Antidotes

Corrective Self-Statements

"Honesty is usually, but not always, the best policy."

"There is such a thing as excessive or compulsive honesty."

"The wrong kind of honesty can be destructive."

"Indiscriminate truths are almost as bad as blatant lies."

"Nobody has to know every single truth about me. I am entitled to some privacy."

"Honesty that hurts others unnecessarily is not a virtue."

Positive Counter-Belief

Total honesty is not the best policy
— love is.

Toxic Idea #11

Inconsiderate Relatives Or Friends Deserve The Silent Treatment

Bennie completely ignored anyone who annoyed him. At times, he would go for weeks without uttering a word to his wife, and if his children misbehaved, he also gave them the "no speaking" treatment. The atmosphere in the home was often as warm, friendly and comfortable as a tomb. At any time, there were at least a half-dozen people with whom he was not on speaking terms. If those who received the "silent treatment" approached him, he would stare right through them and walk away. He was married and divorced four times, and when he died, he died alone.

Analysis

Withdrawing from someone and not speaking to her or him is a form of punishment. "I'll show him!" "That'll teach her!" However, an important, recurring theme throughout this book is that punitive tactics seldom pay off. It certainly makes sense to withdraw from an irksome person who matters very little in your life. But with people who matter — especially loved ones — withdrawal resolves nothing.

Bennie didn't discriminate; he was an "equal opportunity" ignorer. And with people who mattered to him — especially his loved ones — his behavior solved nothing. In fact, Bennie's behavior — ignoring *anyone* who annoyed him — destroyed the potential for loving relationships with his wife and children, not to mention anyone else. By so doing, he intensified his own resentment and that of others. Sulking and dishing out the silent treatment may signal feelings of personal inadequacy. Bennie's behavior — never facing the difficulties in relationships or seeking solutions — was cowardly and immature.

There are indeed some vexatious people who are probably best avoided. After a turbulent one-year marriage, John and Sue got divorced, and they decided to have nothing more to do with each other. If they happened to pass in the street, they would ignore each other completely. Theirs was an irreparable relationship that required no further expenditure of energy.

But if you are interested in pursuing a satisfactory relationship with someone, withdrawing or refusing to converse with the other can only prove destructive. Sally was upset when her only brother did not show up at a family christening. "I'll never speak to him again!" she said. This decision was fine if she genuinely wished to put a permanent end to their relationship, but *only* then.

If you care about someone, withdrawal is one of the least helpful strategies for resolving problems or settling disagreements. With friends, colleagues, co-workers, and especially family members — parents, spouses, children, and other relatives — whenever any problem arises, the wise thing is to *talk it out.*

How to "talk it out"? We recommend the well-known, straightforward guidelines for assertive (as opposed to aggressive) ways to communicate. Janet uses assertive communication when "talking it out" with Frank in the following scenario:

• First, *describe the problem:* "When we had lunch with Mavis and Joel, you excluded me from the conversation. You did the same thing at the Marcus' party. On a few occasions when I tried to get a word in edgewise, you cut me off."

• Next, *state how you feel* about it: "I feel mad and sad because I think I look foolish, and it seems to me that my opinion doesn't mean much to you."

• Then *explain how you would like the situation to be changed:* "I would like it if you stopped brushing me aside. Ideally, it would be great if you would turn to me occasionally and ask, 'What do you think or feel about that?'"

• Finally, *state the probable outcome* of these actions: "This change would please me a great deal, and I'd feel a lot closer to you. I'd also be more willing to go out with you and your friends if this is what you really want."

Notice that Janet wisely avoids using "you are" messages: "You are an inconsiderate and self-centered boor!", for example. "Talking it out" does not mean "rubbing it in" by judging the other person. It means describing the problem from *your* perspective, stating how *you* feel, and explaining how *you* would like the situation to be changed. It pays to confront these issues and to resolve them assertively, not to run away from them.

Antidotes

Corrective Self-Statements

> *"If I don't talk about it, how can I resolve it?"*

> *"Withdrawing from a person or situation is the opposite of problem-solving."*

> *"If the actions of a relative or friend hurt or offend me, the rational, intelligent and mature thing to do is talk it out."*

> *"To solve a problem I will confront it, not avoid it."*

Positive Counter-Belief

> *People you care about deserve communication, not silence.*

You Can Achieve Almost Anything

"If you really want to achieve something, just make up your mind to do it!" advised Bob's father and older brother Ed — both outstanding athletes. While his father and Ed were tall muscular men, Bob had inherited a very slender frame and substandard eye-hand coordination. Bob admired them greatly and wanted to emulate them, but was ill-equipped to do so. Try as he might, he could never develop more than a mediocre physique and unimpressive athletic abilities. "You're just not trying hard enough," his father insisted.

Analysis

Can anyone who wants to *really* become a great basketball player? Can everyone learn to write great literature? Can anyone possess perfect pitch, great visual acuity, or superb manual dexterity?

Perhaps more than any of the other toxic ideas in this book, this misbelief represents the Big Lie in our society. The fact is that all of us have limitations which don't permit us to "achieve almost anything." The barriers may be personal — physical, mental, or emotional shortcomings. Formative environmental events might have prevented the development of expertise in a very wide array of human endeavors. And it gets worse. Despite our laws and beliefs about individual rights, irrational discrimination creates very real obstacles to success — socio-economic, ethnic, religious, gender, age, and/or racial — in any number of fields.

Trying to prove the impossible to yourself and to others is both damaging and a waste of time, yet so many people get locked into pursuing goals that aren't meant to be. One of our patients, the son of a successful attorney, dropped out of law school. Louis found that he was simply not suited to that type of career. He had followed his father's urgings, ignoring his own interests and the fact that he was extraordinarily adroit with his hands. His failure and frustration led him to seek help. In therapy he began to acknowledge his native talents and interests, was encouraged to switch to dentistry, and graduated near the top of his class.

True, we are often told tales about people who achieved miraculous things against great odds. The thin, scrawny guy on the beach who had sand kicked in his face became a bodybuilder and won the "Mr. Universe" contest. The high school dropout who took up art became a famous painter. But it's less glamorous to hear about the millions of people who had set their sights too high and fell flat on their faces. An acquaintance remarked: "If there is one chance in a million, I'll go for it!" We inquired if he frequently bought lottery tickets. "Sure thing!" he answered. Had he ever won anything? "Not yet." This unfortunate mentality has led many impoverished people to squander their money on lottery tickets they could ill afford.

In order to set realistic goals, you need to take an honest inventory of your strengths and weaknesses, your abilities and your limitations. If you find this difficult to do, a formal aptitude test may prove helpful. For example, one of us at age 18 was most interested in architecture, music, acting, and writing. Aptitude testing revealed very poor visual-spatial abilities which effectively ruled out architecture as a career. Musical abilities were above average but decidedly not outstanding. Some intelligent elders and peers pointed out that becoming a successful actor was largely a matter of chance—too risky, too competitive, too filled with unknowns. Verbal and literary skills were high, but becoming a successful writer (as with acting) requires more than simple proficiency. However, the aptitude test, which included an interest schedule, revealed skills and a genuine interest in problem-solving, social concerns, working with people, and a clear inquisitiveness about what makes people tick. The advisor recommended that a career in teaching, law, or psychology be seriously considered.

Realistic assessments — whether formal career guidance or informal self-evaluation — can help you avoid trying to become something or somebody you are not cut out to be. They'll enable you to evaluate your own capacities without fruitlessly striving for the impossible. If you're a good tennis player or golfer, you can try to become even better, but avoid overdoing it. Don't aspire to play at Wimbeldon or at the Masters (unless you are already quite outstanding or exceptional).

You may ask, "Who thinks like that? How many people aim for pie in the sky?" The fact is, we have seen many people "go for broke" and end up hurt if not destroyed by aiming too high. For example, some years ago, the 22-year-old son of one of our friends dropped out of college to form a band. He had grossly overestimated his musical talents and fell flat on his face. We are fairly sure that you can provide similar examples from your own acquaintances.

Many ask, "How will I know what I can and cannot do until I give it my best shot?" Bob, in the original example, deluded himself about being capable of becoming an athlete and experienced frustration and humiliation by marching to the drum of his father and older brother. He would have been far better off pursuing goals that lay within his grasp. Sean was another young man under similar circumstances who did just that. He steered clear of the gym and the sporting fields (his father taught physical education at the local high school) but became a tournament chess and bridge player.

After assessing your interests, abilities, and goals, if you still believe that you can achieve almost anything, it may be that you are not able to take an honest self-inventory. Consider seriously seeking input from an objective outsider. As therapists, we often play this role when our clients are about to bite off more than they can chew.

If a goal lies within your reach, by all means go for it. But if the strain is too much, you need to reassess the situation. Don't try to split a granite rock by banging your head on it! Or, to use a different metaphor, *remember to shift gears.* If your plans are not working out and you are feeling tired, discouraged and frustrated, it's probably time to try something else. Going in a different direction, no longer frustrated by lack of success, you'll grow as a result of the challenge and the pursuit of your passion.

Antidotes

Corrective Self-Statements

> *"To know and admit my limitations is not a sign of failure but of intelligence."*

> *"Impossible dreams often turn into continuous nightmares."*

> *"Those who set out to beat formidable odds often end up with nothing."*

> *"I will assess my own abilities honestly, and then, if the goal lies within my grasp, I will go for it."*

> *"I will not kill myself trying to prove the impossible."*

> *"Why bite off more than I can chew?"*

> *"Knowing what I can't do is as important as knowing what I can."*

Positive Counter-Belief

*You can achieve a great deal
if you set realistic goals
and work toward them diligently.*

If You Want Something Done Right, Do It Yourself

Tony was very handy. Because he was so capable and good with his hands, he insisted on doing all the yard work and any necessary home maintenance and repairs. This put quite a strain on his time, energy and marital relationship. He had a demanding but well-paying job and often brought work home from the office. Still he refused to let someone else assist with or attend to some of his household chores. Weeks often passed before he found time to attend to certain tasks, which created a strain between Tony and his wife. Nonetheless, this incurable do-it-yourselfer remained optimistic: "I'll get it done myself."

Analysis

The do-it-yourself tradition runs deep in the U.S. psyche. Visions of pioneers cutting logs and building cabins in the wilderness haunt our hardware stores and lumber yards on Saturday mornings. Tony has lots of company. Actually, it is often true that if you want to get something done (or done well), your best avenue is to do it yourself. Like any "often truth," however, this attitude can obviously be carried too far. We've met many people whose lives are an endless list of chores, who have virtually no time for leisure and recreation because "the grass needs cutting, the house needs painting, the car needs fixing," and so forth. These are people who can well afford to pay someone else to do the work, but their stinginess or perfectionism makes this possibility unthinkable. Many people, of course, really can't afford to hire someone. Others insist, "I enjoy mowing the lawn; it's good exercise." There are also hobbyists who proudly tell us, "I love tinkering with the car." But we are referring to people who are fairly well-off financially but hard-pressed for time, and yet they compulsively insist on doing things themselves that others could easily have done for them.

These are people — often men — who (1) can't let go of *control* of a project, (2) have big ego investments in saying, "I did it myself," and/or (3) simply don't trust anyone else to handle a job well. They are likely to have trouble delegating at work, too — and backlogs occur there as well. Usually hard-driven "Type A" personalities, this group of independent souls is on a fast-track to undermining their quality of life.

Jack and Ken are next door neighbors who decided that their homes would be enhanced by adding decks. Jack spent the entire summer building his deck himself while Ken hired a contractor and spent most of his time at the shore. There would be no problem if do-it-yourselfer Jack and his family had enjoyed the effort he expended. But he found it tedious and exhausting, and his wife and children resented the fact that he spent hardly any time with them. Jack speaks of the project proudly, but he and his family paid a price for his pride.

Asking for help, delegating responsibility to others, and utilizing the talents of professionals frees you to attend to more important matters and enhances the quality of your life. A friend of ours, with a sense of humor, said: "Never do anything yourself that you can leave to others." Even people who are not financially comfortable can delegate chores, e.g., to teenage children or others in their environment.

One of our patients, a mechanical engineer, complained that whenever she hired workers around the house, the jobs they did were not as good as she could have done herself. When she learned to settle for something "good enough" rather than "perfect," tensions and anxieties that had bothered her for years disappeared. In addition, she had the time for projects she truly enjoyed.

(Related Toxic Idea: #7 "PERFECTION SHOULD BE YOUR GOAL.")

Antidotes

Corrective Self-Statements

> *"Unless I truly enjoy a task, or I'm really the only one who can do it, why bother?"*

> *"What I save in dollars by doing the work*

myself, I might lose in affection by taking time away from family and friends."

"Let me be honest: Am I merely being stingy by refusing to let someone else do it?"

"By delegating responsibility to others, I can free myself for really important matters."

Positive Counter-Belief

*Set priorities,
balance your responsibilities,
do things you like and can do,
delegate more often.*

When Things Go Wrong, Find Someone To Blame

Delia almost always pointed the finger of accusation at others. "Who's to blame for this mess in the kitchen?" "Who's fault is it that we missed the turn in the road?" "Whose mistake cost us a thousand dollars?" This behavior did not endear her to others. When she lost her job, she blamed her boss. When her marriage deteriorated and ended, she accepted no responsibility but blamed her husband.

Analysis

Finding culprits and blaming them is a practice that has led to extreme guilt and unhappiness for many of our patients. An older brother said to his sister, "I blame you for our mother's death. You should have called the doctor

sooner." In this case, the accusation was entirely unfounded, which was perhaps even worse than if it had been
true. But even if her brother had been correct, what was
gained by such a remark?

In essence, blaming has four drawbacks. First, it
doesn't solve the problem. Blaming someone for a real or
imagined misdeed only addresses the *past*: "It's your fault
that Clayton fell off the horse at Grandma's farm." "You
spilled the champagne on Clara's new dress and ruined it."
Problem-solving usually calls for a plan that can be applied
to *future* behaviors: "When you saddle up the horses, try to
make sure that the stirrups are adjusted to the person's
height." "I think it's a good idea to uncork the champagne
over the sink."

Blaming also causes friction. When blamed, most
people go on the defensive. If they feel that the accusation
is unjustified, they will almost certainly counterattack.
Even if they feel guilty as charged, they are nevertheless
apt to try to exonerate themselves. A blaming remark is
inevitably perceived as an attack.

Blamers usually fail to take responsibility for their
own actions. A dispute almost never involves one person
being 100% right and the other, 100% wrong. Chronic
blamers should ask themselves, "Where did *I* go wrong?" or
"How did *I* help to create this problem?" so they can learn
from their mistakes.

Constantly pointing the finger of accusation at others
doesn't lead to mutually accepted responsibility; looking at
the situation objectively does. For example, Stan's assessment of his conflict with Rick does reflect this acceptance:
"In my argument with Rick, I made some uncalled-for
remarks about his wife's short fuse and her sense of humor.
My remarks were silly because they had nothing to do with

the point Rick and I were discussing and only served to sidetrack us. Then Rick made some equally unkind remarks about my sister's divorce. So we both escalated the conflict by not sticking to the point."

Blaming also results in lowered self-esteem (especially in children). Blaming remarks usually convey the following messages: "You're bad." "You're stupid." "You're wrong." "You're nasty." "You're selfish." Most therapists see many patients who heap blame upon themselves for just about everything that goes wrong. In fact, their life histories almost invariably reveal that blaming parents and blaming teachers figured prominently during their formative years.

Blaming, accusing, condemning, chiding or reproaching others or yourself is destructive. In fact, these actions hinder constructive, creative solutions to conflicts. Thus, when things go wrong, one of the most constructive habits to cultivate is to first ask yourself, "How did *I* contribute to this problem?" It's worth repeating that a dispute almost never involves one party being 100% right and the other 100% wrong. Thus, when Dan had a falling out with his supervisor at work and got fired, he blamed the administration, the foreman, the manager — everyone but himself. *We are not advocating self-blame* (which is just as destructive as blaming others). *We're advocating taking responsibility for your actions* in a non-blaming way: "Let me try to see what I could have done differently that might have led to a better outcome."

When things go wrong between you and another person, for both of you to ask, "What can *we* do about it? How can *we* prevent it from happening in the future?" is far more constructive than "Who went wrong and who's to blame?" You've opened channels of communication that will facilitate problem-solving. Compare the following statements: (1) "We lost the tennis match because you kept rushing to the net." (2) "We need to coordinate our base line tactics before moving to the net." Notice that, unlike the first statement, the second attempts to explain what went wrong without finding fault, which will enable both people involved to learn from their mistakes.

Remember that laying blame at anybody's feet (including your own) is only going to discourage a constructive solution. Instead of blaming someone (e.g., "It's your fault that the phone bill is so high!"), it is better to ask for a change in behavior (e.g., "Because the bill is so high, would you try to limit your long-distance calls?").

Antidotes

Corrective Self-Statements

> *"Blaming and fault-finding are aggressive and almost always destructive."*

> *"Instead of blaming somebody, look for a helpful solution."*

> *"Blaming others or yourself is damaging. Instead, determine how to avoid making similar mistakes from now on."*

> *"When you are tempted to point a finger of accusation at someone, first ask yourself if you contributed to the problem."*

Positive Counter-Belief

When things go wrong,
find the problem and solve it.

Punishment Is Good Discipline

Vera was a disciplinarian who ruled her family with an iron hand. Everyone, including her husband, had to be punctual and do the chores Vera assigned without any discussion. Actually, she was inappropriately and needlessly punitive, never for a moment considering her family members' feelings or points of view. Small wonder her children were anxious and beset by numerous emotional problems. Vera's father had been a high ranking naval officer who "ran a tight ship" at work and at home. "Compared to Vera, he was a pussycat!" her husband commented.

Analysis

Punishment will temporarily suppress many unwanted or annoying behaviors. But punitive tactics rarely resolve difficulties or prevent strife; in fact, they often create greater problems. Those being punished, like Vera's husband and children, typically experience alienation, terror, hatred, depression, or other negative effects. They may manage to get back at the offender with sabotage or indirect aggression, escalating the already-painful cycle of strife. Let's face it, punishment — whether the victim is being censured, chastised, rebuked, scolded, or worse yet, beaten — engenders anything but love.

The I'll-teach-you-a-lesson philosophy that accompanies harsh punishment only ends up teaching the recipient to be violent, harsh, abusive, vicious, or else submissive. Punishment causes alienation and resolves nothing; it is a primitive, inferior way of teaching a lesson whose goal is to intimidate, bully, and harass someone into "behaving or else." What's more, no one benefits; in fact, everyone loses.

If you fail to take action when your child misbehaves, you will make it difficult for the child to develop appropriate behaviors and ultimately, to be self-disciplined. But the old cliché, "Spare the rod and spoil the child" is dead wrong. Desirable, appropriate, prosocial behavior results from proper coaching, teaching, and role modeling, not from "rods." People (and nations) would do well to educate, enlighten, and instruct rather than to intimidate and retaliate.

When your goal is to educate in order to solve problems or to correct your child's negative behavior, rewarding positive behavior is the most likely method of achieving this goal. In fact, a wealth of psychological re-search shows that rewarding positive responses (rather than punishing negative ones) greatly enhances learning. Catch your child being "good," and reward her. Let toddler Susan know how proud you are that she told you she had to go to the toilet; don't punish her because she waited too long. Tell eight-year-old Jonathan what a good job he did cleaning his room — even if it wouldn't pass G.I. inspection. When Carmen comes home from her date 20 minutes past curfew, thank her for calling to let you know she'd be late.

As parents, you will raise happier, more cooperative children if you reward them for positive actions or for refraining from negative ones, instead of punishing them for "bad behavior." For your ultimate goal is to teach your children to develop self-discipline, which will enable them to become independent, well-adjusted, happy adults.

Antidotes

Corrective Self-Statements

> *"Positive reinforcement pays off; punishment usually creates greater problems."*

> *"It is better to discipline children kindly and lovingly than to punish them."*

> *"At best, punishment will only temporarily suppress an annoying behavior."*

> *"It is better to educate than to intimidate."*

"Most people learn far more from kind words than from harsh ones."

Positive Counter-Belief

Instead of punishing others for bad deeds, catch them being good and reward them.

Keep Your Feelings To Yourself

Earl kept most of his thoughts and feelings to himself. His father used to say: "Even a fish wouldn't get into trouble if it kept its mouth shut!" He was raised to believe that if other people were not in on your opinions or feelings, they couldn't hurt you or take advantage of you. But Earl complained bitterly that he often felt "awfully lonely."

Analysis

Earl is one of the many people who believe that it's clever to be enigmatic, a puzzle to others: "The less anyone knows about you, the better." Untrue! And it's often an untruth with sad consequences. There can be no genuine love or truly close friendships without personal revelations, without shared intimacies and confidences. Naturally, there are situations in which it is wise to conceal your innermost feelings from others, but when you make it a way of life to hide your values and feelings, you end up emotionally and spiritually arid.

People who carry a guarded attitude into their marriages, friendships and other personal encounters miss out on much of the joy that comes from sincere sharing and a sense of belonging. They guarantee themselves a lonely and detached existence. Moreover, one of the best ways to acquire self-knowledge is by revealing yourself to others.

We don't deny that there may be risks in self-disclosure. There are a few people who may try to use shared confidences against you, but it's usually not difficult to sense who is for you and who shouldn't be given the time of day; to whom you can reveal your innermost thoughts, feelings and actions, and who is potentially treacherous. To go through life hiding behind a façade because there's a chance some adversary may use information against you is most unfortunate and misguided. To deprive yourself of the richness of intimate, loving and supportive relationships by constantly hiding from others will lead you to feel alienated from yourself.

Many people proclaim with great pride, "I'm a very private person." What's so admirable about that? Being too private can be just as bad as being too public. We have all met blabbermouths who tell us their complete life histories at a first meeting, revealing intimate details that most people would prefer not to hear. The impenetrable and opaque shields that certain "very private people" erect are just as bad. Even close associates and family can feel shut out, alienated and excluded. Earl and the many people like him who subscribe to this misbelief tend to wall themselves off so effectively that they experience a type of solitary confinement. Is it fear, shame, guilt, or suspicion that leads these people to conceal their true feelings from those closest to them?

If you want to maintain intimate relationships with your family and friends, we urge you to talk about your actions and confide your feelings and thoughts to them. Be selective; don't tell everything to everyone. Begin slowly, and choose those you know are worthy of your trust. Then risk being more open and self-disclosing (selectively, of course) and see how your relationships become more satisfying. Resolve not to hide your honest opinions, without overdoing it.

It's not healthy to bury your true feelings or to suppress your basic emotions. While we don't suggest you "spill your guts" to all and sundry, if you become more open with trusted intimates, you will not regret it.

(Related Toxic Idea: #10 "TOTAL HONESTY IS THE BEST POLICY")

Antidotes

Corrective Self-Statements

"If I'm a mystery to others, I'll probably remain a puzzle to myself."

"Close friendships rest on personal revelations and shared information."

"Selective self-disclosure builds intimacy."

"If I am accepted as people think I am, rather than as I really am, I'll feel phony and insecure."

"Very private people live in emotional prisons they create for themselves."

"Constantly hiding your true feelings from others disconnects you from yourself."

Positive Counter-Belief

Build trust and intimacy
by expressing your feelings.

Toxic Idea #17

First Impressions Tell You What People Are Really Like

Dennis met Claire at his sister's wedding and was very attracted to her. A few weeks later, he invited her to join him for dinner with two other couples. Claire was so quiet throughout the evening that Dennis lost interest in her then and there. "She's a non-person," he told his sister Nancy, "a complete bore!" Nancy, who knew Claire very well, assured Dennis that her friend was usually very lively and vivacious. Maybe that evening Claire had suffered from one of her occasional low-grade migraine headaches, and thus, she'd been somewhat withdrawn, Nancy suggested. Dennis didn't buy it. He persisted in believing that Claire's behavior at the dinner party must be typical.

Analysis

Whenever you generalize about a person — jump to conclusions based on limited exposure — you are likely to be wrong. "Alice is a very selfish person," Kenny declared. "How do you know?" he was asked. "Well, when I asked to her for help with my term paper, she decided that a tennis lesson was more important." It is true that Alice at times makes self-indulgent choices, but only *at times*. Most of the time she could be described as unselfish, and, in fact, she is often quite generous and accommodating. Kenny thought he had Alice figured out; he was wrong.

Many behaviors are situation-specific or person-specific. In the company of her parents and older siblings, Gina was inclined to regress and act childishly, but in virtually all other contexts she acted in an appropriately mature way. Tom was generally easy-going and good humored, but around his Uncle Bill, he became sarcastic, nasty and aggressive. Tom realized that "Uncle Bill brings out the worst in me," but Uncle Bill concluded erroneously that Tom was "an obnoxious person" all the time.

If you really want to draw valid and reliable inferences about someone, you need to observe a representative range of his or her behaviors in a wide variety of situations. Before concluding, "He is selfish." "She is shy." You must ask "*How* selfish, or *how* shy, and under *what circumstances, with whom*, on which specific occasions?" "Is he sometimes decidedly unselfish?" "Is she ever positively un-shy?" You'll be fairer to others and to yourself if you think and act on the basis of *evidence*, without drawing final conclusions until you have sufficient data and clear-cut facts to justify them.

(Related Toxic Idea: #36 "YOU WON'T GO WRONG IF YOU FOLLOW YOUR GUT FEELINGS.")

Antidotes
Corrective Self-Statements

"I don't know her very well."

"I've only seen him a couple of times."

"He may have had a really bad day when I saw him."

"Nobody is the same in all circumstances."

"Do I really know the whole story?"

"What else was going on when I saw her acting that way?"

"Could there be a problem about which I am unaware?"

"Have I asked enough questions to check out my assumptions?"

"Dig for facts rather than jump to conclusions."

Positive Counter-Belief

*Every individual is unique;
you don't know what a person is "really like"
unless you have seen him or her
in different circumstances.*

Your Parents' Approval Is Most Important

Roger describes his quest for his parents' approval in this way: "When I turned 35 I realized that almost everything I had done in life was intended to please my parents, especially my father. I was always their favorite kid and went out of my way to make them proud of me. When I finished high school I went to a college my dad picked, and afterward I followed his wishes and went to business school. By the time I was 30, I was married, had two kids, and was earning big money, but I was miserable, and eventually I tried to kill myself. I realized I wasn't leading my own life; I was merely following my dad's script. I had married Dora because my parents liked her, not because I really loved her.... So although my parents strongly disapproved, I got a divorce, moved out of state, went to medical school and started leading my own life, marching to my own drummer."

Analysis

Many people, young and old, believe that they have to live up to their parents' expectations, to earn their parents' approval. But, as Roger learned, that's not a healthy way to live your life. Quite to the contrary, it's best if you zealously refuse to live up to *anybody's* expectations (and it is wise not to impose your expectations on others either). Your parents face many things they dislike but are powerless to do anything about — pollution, crime, taxes, inflation. It's unrealistic to think that they or anyone else could approve of everything you do, just as you surely do not approve of all of their actions and attitudes. Perhaps the most realistic goal is parental *acceptance,* not approval.

Even parents who truly love and adore their grown children and want the best for them, are misguided if they expect the children to live their lives in accordance with *anyone* else's needs. Because his father made it clear that he was to attend medical school, Joel earned an M.D. from a prestigious university. However, instead of continuing to fulfill his father's dream that he become a surgeon and earn a fortune, Joel decided to go into research. He became an outstanding medical scientist and author and was in charge of a major laboratory, but nonetheless considered himself "a failure in life" because his salary was much lower than his classmates earned from private practice. Had he won the Nobel Prize (which includes a large monetary award), his father would have approved. He didn't however, and thus continued to feel that he had let his father down.

You and your parents will get along best when they realize that your life needs to unfold the way *you* want it to, without interference from them. Naturally, there is no harm in seeking guidance from your parents and others, but in the final analysis, you need to do what *you* really feel is best. If your parents disapprove of you or your lifestyle, that's their choice; you're not a puppet whose strings they must control. Surely, it is better when children and parents see eye-to-eye, and when genuine love and mutual respect form the foundation for the adult parent-child relationship. Unfortunately, this mutuality is often impossible to attain. You may regret that, but you must get on with *your* life. You may have to go against your parents' wishes if you want to be fulfilled. If you lead your life in order to please them, to win their love and approval, you aren't truly living at all.

Antidotes

Corrective Self-Statements

> *"I am not on this earth to live up to anyone's expectations."*

> *"I will live my own life, not somebody else's."*

> *"I will learn to write my own script and march to my own drummer."*

> *"I would prefer to have my parents' approval, but I don't need it in order to be happy."*

> *"I do not have to upset myself if my parents disapprove of what I do or who I am."*

> *"It is better to respect and admire myself than to try to fit someone else's image of me."*

Positive Counter-Belief

*Parental approval is desirable
but not necessary for personal fulfillment.*

Success And Money
Lead To Happiness

As far back as he could remember, Peter had his heart set on making money. Even as a child he was materialistic and used to come up with ideas, strategies and systems for turning a profit. He worked very hard, graduated from one of the finest business schools, and soon owned a successful chain of hardware stores. He was appointed to the board of directors of several large companies. Peter exemplified the "work very hard and make lots of money" tradition. But there was one major snag. Peter was not happy. In his quest for money and recognition, he had failed to devote time to cultivating close, loving relationships.

Analysis

Though Peter had achieved the fame and fortune (but not the happiness) he had set out to attain, many people work themselves to death and fail to make money or to achieve significant status or recognition. Work addictions (e.g., workaholism) are almost as unhealthy as chemical addictions (e.g., alcoholism). How many people work themselves to the bone planning to accumulate enough money to really enjoy life once they retire, only to die, or become too ill to reap the benefits of their very hard work?

Indeed, work achievements and material rewards cannot buy happiness. Working hard makes sense. So does striving to make enough money to pay for necessities, and with prudence and good luck, some luxuries. In fact, hard work can often be intrinsically rewarding; it is satisfying when your employers and colleagues recognize and appreciate your efforts and achievements. Indeed, the "drop out" philosophy is not the antidote to the toxic idea that success and money lead to happiness — it's merely the opposite extreme. But unless you are one of the few fortunate people whose career is profoundly engaging and meaningful, try to view work and money as means to ends rather than as ends in themselves. As one philosopher put it, "The highest reward for our toil is not what we get for it but what we become by it."

You are much more likely to be enriched and fulfilled if you "invest" in human "commodities," such as nurturing relationships with family and friends, loving, sharing, and enjoying the simple pleasures of life, rather than acquiring great wealth and material things, the external evidence of "success."

One of the happiest people we know is a man who worked for most of his life in a grocery store. Because his family had been too poor to allow him to finish high school, Tom had to start working at age 14. Twelve years later, he happily married Eloise. Together they lived in a modest house, made ends meet and had three lovely children. Tom left plenty of time to enjoy his family, take up hobbies, nurture close friendships, and have fun. Today, at age 83, Tom derives great joy from his relationship with his wife, children, grandchildren, and great grandchildren. If Peter could trade places with him, he'd come out ahead! The rich and famous are not automatically happy.

One of our friends told us a poignant story that had helped him realize how important, indeed, how priceless, close relationships are. He had grown up in an exceedingly wealthy family and lived in a huge mansion with indoor and outdoor tennis courts and swimming pools. From his bedroom window, looking across many acres of their property, he could see little houses. "Who lives in those houses?" he inquired. "Poor people," his mother answered. Then she went on to describe the misery of these people's lives. But our friend discovered something entirely different: "When I was six or seven I got a bicycle, and for the first time, I rode past the poor people's houses. I heard laughter coming from one of them and wondered what these unfortunate people could possibly find to laugh about. Later, I became friendly with one of the boys who lived on that street, despite my parents' displeasure about our friendship. The first time I had dinner at his house, I saw and felt the love and family togetherness that had been absent in our own home. My parents were literally too busy to pay attention to little else except counting their millions, whereas his family shared a special closeness I had never experienced.

Although I was only about seven years old, I realized that relationships matter far more than money."

Antidotes
Corrective Self-Statements

> *"There's more to life than making money."*

> *"Wealth is no guarantee of happiness."*

> *"People who have the love of family and friends are the truly 'wealthy' ones."*

> *"A millionaire who does not receive genuine love and caring is emotionally impoverished."*

> *"Work to live; don't live to work."*

> *"Your true worth cannot be measured by your wealth."*

Positive Counter-Belief

Loving relationships lead to happiness.

Once A Victim, Always A Victim

Carol is entering her tenth year of psychoanalysis. She had an unhappy childhood, occasioned by her father's domination and her mother's long-standing "martyrdom." The only girl in a family of five, she felt that her brothers received love and respect from her parents, whereas she was neglected and ignored. She claims that her brothers were seldom kind to her. "I'll probably never get over these hurts," she declared. She is 43.

Analysis

Psychologically, your life history and your genetic programming are the bases for the development of your personality. The effects of childhood experiences can clearly exist well into adulthood; you tend to repeat old behavior patterns. But most of these effects do not lock you in the past unless you give them the power to do so and you continue to dwell on them.

Carol has allowed the past to wield enormous power over her, not realizing that the past is gone and does not have a magical impact on her present or future. As a child, Carol was unable to stand up to her somewhat abusive and domineering father. Thirty-plus years later, she still feels bound to remain subservient.

Many people raised in unhappy homes continue to feel powerless and bad. Twenty-three-year-old Becky put it this way: "How can I ever get to feel good about myself? After all, I'm an ACOA!" (Adult Child of an Alcoholic). Those who have been beaten repeatedly or sexually abused as children often become prisoners of the past as well.

But people *can* undo the damaging effects of the past. Even in the most severe cases, evidence shows that one need not remain victimized and crippled by the past, especially when sensitive professional help is sought. Some habits and feelings may be hard to overcome — hard but not impossible. There is hope.

If, like Carol, you don't challenge faulty notions and instead, accept them as truths about yourself, you won't be able to free yourself from the painful past. You need to learn new problem-solving tactics here-and-now, to challenge the old "truths" and notions.

Predictably, if you were belittled as a child, your mind has recorded all of those humiliations and plays them back frequently. This negative "self-talk," for the most part, then, has resulted in many negative feelings. Changing your self-talk from negative to positive really helps to transform your negative *feelings* to positive ones. In fact, one of the most effective forms of psychotherapy, cognitive therapy, is largely based on the powerful effects of changing what you tell yourself. If you tell yourself often enough that you'll fail, you perhaps will fail or at least feel inadequate to succeed before you ever try. But if you tell yourself that you'll succeed, you will dramatically improve your chances of making it. Simpleminded? Perhaps. But positive statements powerfully and effectively create positive feelings, especially when combined with deliberate attempts to act in accordance with your desires.

Here is one technique to change your negative self-talk. First, list every putdown you can recall ever being directed at you. Then, taking these negative comments one by one, examine their accuracy. See if there is any factual basis for them. This exercise requires a little time and effort, because repeated examination and challenge is what leads to change. Even if in the past you have done some stupid, hurtful, or foolish things, they would not have made you a stupid, hurtful, or foolish *person*. Catch yourself putting yourself down with negative remarks like these: "I fail at everything I do," "Why bother? I can't do anything right," "I'm a complete idiot," "I'm a total incompetent," "I don't deserve to be happy." Replace these putdowns over and over again with positive statements: "I'm pretty smart," "I do quite well," "I'm a good salesperson," "I can be interesting and a lot of fun," "I hope I get a raise, but if I don't, I'll get over it." Keep your positive statements realistic —

it won't help to lie to yourself — but avoid self-critical remarks and focus on the plus-side.

In addition to counteracting negative self-talk, actively dispute the belief that you are forever trapped by your past. One effective technique is to think about specific unhappy childhood experiences while you are deeply relaxed and to repeat a statement such as, "This is history. It's long gone. I am now an adult." You might try visualization techniques as well. Imagine painful incidents from childhood and visualize the people who hurt you being shrunk to the size of ants, for example. If repeated over and over, these exercises often take the sting out of past traumas. Many people report that they emerge feeling empowered.

Your future behavior will be based on your actions today. What you do today will become your past tomorrow. Thus, a combination of determined rethinking, visualization practice, and new, effective actions (e.g., forcing yourself to behave like an assertive adult even if your knees are shaking) can release you from the agony of the past. If, over time, you consistently change negative self-talk into positive self-affirmation, and practice acting assertively, this new mode of thought and action will become a basic part of your personality. In the process, you will transform past defeats into present and future fulfillment.

Antidotes

Corrective Self-Statements

> *"The past is gone; I can and will let go of it."*

> *"I'm an adult now, not a frightened child."*

> *"Past hurts don't have to haunt me forever."*

"I will not dwell needlessly on what was; instead, I will focus on what is and what can be."

"I will act like an assertive adult even if at times I feel like a scared child."

"If I catch myself putting myself down, I will practice rephrasing what I say, substituting positive terms for negative ones."

Positive Counter-Belief

You can free yourself from past hurts.

Be Modest; Don't Flatter Yourself

Jim was an exceedingly bright, capable and talented young research assistant who considered it crude and boorish to "blow your own horn." Consequently, he was so reserved and self-effacing in social situations, he came across as lacking in self-confidence. On the job, he undersold himself to such an extent that fellow workers far less capable received promotions over him. His motto, "My work speaks for itself," earned him few rewards other than modest self-satisfaction. In his personal life, he lacked the confidence to approach women he found attractive and remained lonely enough to seek help in therapy.

Analysis

The way you present and "package" yourself has a tremendous impact on how others perceive you. Any extreme, be it excessive modesty or exorbitant boastfulness, will usually prove self-destructive. False modesty often breeds resentment in others and, as Jim learned painfully, isolation and loneliness.

When Sam asked Ned if he was a strong tennis player, Ned replied: "I'm kind of average." In truth, Ned was a very strong player who had won several tournaments. When Ned proceeded to blow Sam off the court, Sam concluded that his opponent had lied in order to show him up. All Ned needed to say was that he was indeed a strong player. This is not being immodest. Compare that statement with this one: "Are you kidding? I'm a fantastic player. My serve usually comes in at over 100 miles an hour. I'm an undefeated champion of three divisions and probably the best in the state." Now *that* would be offensive — unless he was joking. We all realize that bragging and showing off are signs of insecurity, and that most people are repulsed by this sort of behavior. Because many individuals think in terms of dichotomies, they assume that someone is either modest or arrogant. Since they correctly believe that it is in poor taste to brag or be boastful, they assume that undue modesty is their best option.

But there is a middle ground. It is best to be appropriately honest, to openly admit your strengths without flaunting them. You needn't hide your talents nor boast of them immodestly. Acknowledge your abilities instead of minimizing or denying them; you'll avoid misunderstandings and needless rejection, and you may gain recognition and rewards.

If false modesty has led you to undersell yourself, don't be surprised if you've been "lost in the shuffle," and/or passed over at work. If there are things you do well, or if you have a certain degree of knowledge or expertise, you are well-advised to let your talents and abilities be known. Undue modesty will get you no farther than will vanity, arrogance, or conceit. Simply declare yourself and your abilities, not through boastful rhetoric or self-aggrandizement, but through appropriate disclosure and demonstration of your skills.

Antidotes

Corrective Self-Statements

> *"There is a middle ground between being extremely boastful or unduly modest."*

> *"Openly stating my strengths and abilities is not the same as 'blowing my own horn.' "*

> *"False modesty is dishonest and can have negative results."*

> *"It is usually best to declare my capabilities without flaunting them."*

> *"If I am good at something and say so, I am simply being sincere, not egotistical."*

Positive Counter-Belief

Openly and honestly declare your strengths and abilities.

Criticism Is A Good Way To Correct People's Mistakes

Howard freely admitted that he was "very critical." He owned a market research firm, and in the space of one year, he hired eight secretaries for the same position; most quit within a month. He also had three failed marriages and no close friends. Howard saw himself as "a decent, reasonable guy with high standards." He could not understand why almost everyone whom he encountered turned out to be so thin-skinned. "How can people learn unless you actively criticize them?" he asked.

Analysis

Learning from mistakes is the basis of education and growth. Other people's comments can steer us in the right direction. The danger lies in making generalized negative comments to describe people's traits and personalities. "You're stupid!" is the type of criticism that can only alienate. It is usually detrimental to criticize a *person* rather than to comment on a *specific action*.

Criticism of a person (rather than the correction of a specific action) most often ruptures relationships. Criticism damages self-esteem, devalues and dehumanizes the recipient, leads to defensiveness, causes resentment, focuses on difficulties rather than on solutions, and creates rather than resolves conflicts.

To belittle someone, to resort to scorn, mockery, ridicule, or derision in the name of "constructive criticism," is bound to cause problems. Most people do not like being told what to do or what's wrong with them. Critical parents tend to breed neurotic children — they make money for psychiatrists. Critical spouses generate resentment — they make money for divorce lawyers.

In daily life, you inevitably encounter situations and events that displease you. People make mistakes; they act thoughtlessly or selfishly at times; they forget certain things; and they don't always act as you might wish them to. At these times, you may feel compelled to comment, to offer advice, to point out their errors. When doing so, if you are harsh or critical, if you resort to sarcasm or ridicule, chances are that all you will achieve is to offend them.

Unless carefully worded and sensitively presented, critical remarks will not only fail to solve problems, but will actually aggravate them. When conflicts arise, instead of criticizing the offender, look for solutions; think up specific problem-solving tactics.

Here's a vignette that should clarify the point:

Aaron was extremely irritated whenever Melanie, his 17-year-old daughter, forgot to set the burglar alarm when leaving the house. He and his wife typically left the house around 7:00 a.m. Melanie, around 8:00. Despite a break-in two months earlier that resulted in the loss of certain valuables, Melanie was in such a hurry to make the 8:15 bus that she dashed out of the house, only to remember too late that she had not turned on the alarm. "This drives me crazy!" Aaron told his wife, who agreed with the sentiment.

Are these parents best advised to criticize their daughter, calling her stupid, forgetful, scatter-brained, self-centered and irresponsible? Should they accuse her of deliberately setting out to annoy them? Is there any virtue in threatening to "ground" her or withhold her allowance if she fails to activate the alarm in the future? To our way of thinking, each of those "solutions" is only likely to intensify the problem and create additional difficulties.

Aaron wisely asked Melanie if she agreed that it was necessary to switch on the burglar alarm whenever the house was unoccupied. (A "no" response would have called for further discussion about the matter and might have explained her failure to bother with the alarm.) She agreed it was important to do so but declared that she is often distracted and absent-minded in the morning. Aaron's solution was simple but effective. After verifying that Melanie invariably left by the side door, he stuck a bright red-lettered sign IS THE ALARM ON? in plain view above the door knob. That sign solved the problem.

Totally avoiding situations in which you dislike what someone has said or done is impossible. If you want a constructive solution, you need to be careful about what you say and particularly careful about how you say it. Compare these two statements: (1) "You are selfish." (2) "I think it would have been nice if you had shared your cake with Tommy." Notice how the second statement has few judgmental overtones? It also provides a path for corrective action.

The basic formula is to *ask for a change in behavior rather than to attack the person.* Thus, "I hate the way you yell at the kids," would be replaced by "I'd prefer that in the future you didn't holler at the children." A remark such as, "Who do you think I am, your servant or your slave?" is better changed to "I'd really like it if you cleaned and rinsed your plates after dinner and put them in the dishwasher." By developing a habit of commenting about habits or behaviors that you would like to see modified in the future, instead of assailing the person, you are likely to benefit the other person and yourself.

Antidotes

Corrective Self-Statements

> *"Before correcting someone, I need to stop and think how best to do it."*

> *"Scorn, mockery, sarcasm and snide remarks are the opposite of constructive criticism."*

> *"It is best to ask for a change in the person's behavior rather than to criticize the person."*

> *"If I were in the other person's place, how would I like someone to talk to me?"*

Positive Counter-Belief

*Focus on problem solving,
not criticizing past mistakes.*

Toxic Idea #23

Don't Be Selfish; Put Others First

Doris believed that honorable, decent and considerate people do not put their own needs before those of others, especially when dealing with loved ones. She thought that only selfish people who failed to care about the feelings and wishes of others would ever put their own desires first. However, she often felt that her relatives and friends took unfair advantage of her and did not repay her in kind. Inwardly, she usually felt resentful but never expressed her feelings. Many of her friends regarded her as "a bit of a martyr."

Analysis

Doris didn't understand the vast difference between *selfishness* (satisfying your own needs at the expense of others) and *enlightened self-interest* (looking after yourself, but not at the cost of others). In the long run, her own interests are best served by taking into consideration the needs of others, and thinking about others who benefit when she takes care of herself.

There are three possible approaches: 1. Consider yourself first and foremost and, if necessary, trample over others to get what you want. (Those who operate according to this prescription often end up in serious trouble.) 2. Always put others before yourself. (Such a degree of unselfishness also results in unhappy outcomes.) 3. Care for and about yourself, but take others into account. (This is clearly the best alternative.) You fulfill your obligations to others but are prepared to defend, pursue or promote what you believe to be your reasonable rights.

Related to the statements above is the notion that it is better to give than to receive. Why? This mistaken idea has led many people to be extremely ungracious about accepting things from others. Often, another person may derive pleasure from giving or doing something for you, but if you are reluctant or unwilling to accept it, the giver may feel rejected. The point is that neither giving nor receiving is better. It is best to give *and* to receive.

We are not denying that a life of service can be a very good thing. Our point is that *nourishing yourself helps you to be able to give to others*. If you are too self-demeaning, you are only going to make those you serve feel uncomfortable. Indeed, if you are excessively self-effacing, utterly selfless, some may even become contemptuous. For example, everyone agreed that Annie was extremely kind and well-meaning, yet many found her level of philanthropic devotion annoying. She was forever doing things for others, expecting nothing in return. Someone to whom Annie had been extremely helpful remarked, "She's a good soul but a real pain in the neck!" Another person echoed those feelings: "She's an angel; I wish she'd grow wings and fly away."

Annie did not allow give and take. She wanted nothing except to give to others, to serve them, and to do things for them. Whenever anyone asked Annie, "How can I repay you? What can I do for you in return?" she answered, "I don't want anything in return." Most people dislike and resent feeling beholden. Had Annie responded, "You can make a donation to my favorite charity" or "Would you mind spending an hour one day next week in one of our soup kitchens?" people would most likely have come away feeling grateful rather than resentful and incensed over her extremely good intentions.

The presumed virtue of always putting others first, of constantly turning the other cheek is often supported by the widely-quoted saying, "The meek shall inherit the earth." A highly respected clergyman pointed out to us many years ago that this saying, as well as the description of Jesus Christ as "meek and mild," are quite wrong and were handed down through faulty translation. As the clergyman pointed out, the expression "meek and mild" evokes the image of a nonentity, of someone who would let sleeping dogs lie, fail to say "boo!" to the proverbial goose, and avoid trouble whenever possible — in short, uninspired and uninspiring. Yet as the pastor underscored, Jesus Christ is more accurately portrayed as a man who did not hesitate to challenge and expose hypocrisies, a man who could be moved to violent anger by shameless exploitation or by smug orthodoxy. "The embarrassingly wrong picture of sweet tenderness combined with soft sentimentality could easily be put in its proper place by an intelligent reading of the Gospels," the clergyman asserted. And he added that the correct phrase is not "The meek shall inherit the earth," but *"The wise should inherit the earth."* And the wise person fully realizes that if he acts like a doormat, others will simply wipe their feet on him.

Thus, when Sam suggested to his friends that they all go out to a fish restaurant for dinner, was Billy being selfish by saying that since he is allergic to seafood, he would prefer to eat elsewhere? If he had selflessly gone along with the crowd and simply eaten rolls and butter, would this make him a better person? Emphatically not!

Antidotes

Corrective Self-Statements

"I'll look after myself and also consider others."

"Enlightened self-interest is not the same as selfishness."

"My own wishes and desires are just as important as anyone else's."

"If I constantly put others' needs first, neither my needs nor theirs will be fulfilled."

"I will defend what I believe to be my reasonable rights."

"It is best to give and to receive."

Positive Counter-Belief

Care for yourself as you care for others.

Toxic Idea #24

Your Spouse Should Love Your Parents And Family

Doug, an extremely devoted son, was also very close to his two younger sisters. When he married Betsy, he assumed that she would also love and adore his family. Actually, Betsy was not especially fond of her two sisters-in-law, whom she found self-centered and demanding. She was also perturbed that Doug's parents tended to be controlling and interfering. She was always polite, friendly and gracious with her in-laws, but clearly she did not love them. Although Doug admitted that Betsy was warm and friendly to his family, he found her lack of deep love for them unacceptable, and they were divorced within a year.

Analysis

You cannot legislate anyone's feelings. Indeed, to assume that you can tell another person what to feel is absurd. Your feelings and emotions are governed by complex reactions to many situations and events, past and present, and these emotions are your own. One of the great freedoms in life, one that cannot be taken away, is your right to your own feelings. Isn't it foolhardy and self-destructive to try to take away that right from those you love? A mature marriage relationship can't be based on the condition that your spouse love your parents and family. A command such as, "You must love my mom and dad," is beyond reason, however desirable it may be for your spouse to deeply love your parents and siblings. If you try to dictate your partner's feelings, negative results are inevitable.

Does this mean you must allow all forms of abuse toward your family? Certainly not. Though it's useless to tell other people how you think they should *feel*, you can inform them how you would like them to *act*. For example, you may ask for specific behaviors: "Please be pleasant to my parents," or "I want you to treat my parents well." These are entirely reasonable requests.

Clive and Barbara have successfully incorporated this advice into their relationship with Barbara's family. Barbara was inordinately fond of her parents, but Clive didn't even really like them. Knowing of his wife's strong loyalties, he wisely did not verbalize his negative feelings, and he always treated his in-laws with respect. Barbara could sense that her husband was not particularly fond of her parents, but she realized that what counted was not how he *felt* toward them, but the manner in which he *dealt* with them. Of course, when genuine affection and caring exist within the extended family, marital relationships are enriched. But in a healthy marriage, the bond of love between you and your spouse is not dependent on your spouse's feelings about your family members. You certainly can try to make it easier for your spouse to have positive feelings about your relatives, but you can only reasonably expect your spouse to see your family on occasion and to *behave* in a pleasant way. Incidentally, don't forget that your family also has a role in shaping the behavior *and* engendering the positive feelings you would like to see in your spouse. If they want to be *liked,* they'll need to be *likable!*

Antidotes

Corrective Self-Statements

> *"My relationship with my spouse is of primary importance."*

> *"There is an enormous difference between feelings and behavior."*

> *"It is reasonable to ask my partner in a pleasant way for more positive actions toward my family."*

> *"Even though I may love my family, my spouse chose me as a partner, not them."*

> *"I will appreciate what my partner does for my family rather than focus on what he or she does not do."*

Positive Counter-Belief

My partner can treat my family with respect; s/he doesn't have to love them.

Toxic Idea #25

*We All Do Our Best
When We Have High Expectations*

*Brad was a tough-but-good army sergeant.
He was a dependable role model and had
extremely high expectations for his men and
for himself. His platoon suffered fewer
casualties than most, probably because they
were so well-trained. But when Brad
returned to civilian life working as a factory
supervisor, he ran into trouble. He continued
to have very high expectations for those who
worked under him, but the factory was not
the army, and he didn't have the authority to
enforce his will. He was viewed as a source of
stress and his subordinates presented upper
management with a signed petition asking
that he be replaced.*

Analysis

This toxic idea differs from #7 (PERFECTION SHOULD BE YOUR GOAL), which discusses objective standards, levels of performance, and degrees of achievement some people demand. Thus, if Brad were a perfectionist as the factory supervisor, he would have insisted that his workers turn out perfect products, and that the imperfect wares be redone.

But Brad's problem was different. High expectations need *not* be tied to achievement or performance. Brad expected the employees to start work on time, to avoid dallying around the coffee pot, and to observe the proper lunch breaks. He cut his workers little slack. He was not a stickler for perfection, but his rigid expectations landed him in hot water.

Janice *expected* her husband to remember her birthday and their wedding anniversary as well as the birthdays and anniversaries of her three sisters. Robert's *expectations* to become the manager of his division were aimed at himself, and he made himself miserable when failing to live up to his own strict standards. Because Abe *expected* other people to be punctual, he became irate when they kept him waiting. Sally was deeply hurt when her son and daughter-in-law did not invite her for Christmas; she had *expected* to be invited.

In truth, the fewer expectations you have, the less upset and disappointed you will be. One wise individual remarked: "I try not to expect anything from anyone. That way, I rarely feel hurt, upset, let down, disillusioned or disappointed. When nice things happen, I am pleasantly surprised. I have also learned not to expect too much from myself."

These statements should not be misconstrued to suggest that it's good for you to be cynical or to assume a cabbage-like indifference to life, unaffected by the actions of others. There are ethics, morals and standards worth upholding, but problems stem from having unrealistic expectations or too many yearnings. There seems to be little doubt that the more expectations you have, the more letdowns and unhappiness you will experience. And even if you succeed in forcing others to meet your unrealistic expectations, you will probably damage and perhaps destroy your relationship with them.

It's inevitable for you have certain expectations, for yourselves and others. But you need to ask whether any of these expectations are unrealistic or excessive. The more you are able to identify and let go of frivolous demands, and the less you "lay trips" on yourself and others, the better your life will be. Thus, the distinction between *desires* and *demands* is most important. Though it's fine to express your wishes and desires, it's a serious mistake to change them into orders or demands.

In the final analysis, the key question to ask yourself is whether you are being unreasonable in your desires and expectations. If there is any doubt in your mind, ask a close friend to give you an objective opinion.

Antidotes

Corrective Self-Statements

"I will accept myself for what I am."

"If I wish to strive for self-betterment, I'll do so without making unreasonable demands on myself."

"I will be a success by being what I 'can' be, not what I 'must' be."

"It's best to treat myself and others as the fallible human beings we all are."

"I will ask myself if my expectations of others are reasonable or too demanding."

Positive Counter-Belief

We all do our best
when we have reasonable expectations.

It's Important To Be Liked By Everyone

Dave went out of his way to please everybody. He believed that by doing so, everyone would like and respect him. If he sensed that someone disliked him, or if anyone was critical of or nasty to him, he literally lost sleep over it. He was very frank: "I can't stand it when someone dislikes me!" He was devastated when he learned that his nickname around the office was "wimp."

Analysis

Just about everyone likes an innocuous "nice guy." Why dislike someone who amounts to very little, who poses no challenge or threat? Dave wasn't what you'd call "well-liked," but everybody in the office accepted him well enough. When you stand for something, however, dissenters who hold different views are not apt to be so affable. If you define yourself as a unique individual, or if you take a position on virtually any issue, you're bound to have critics and detractors.

Logically, rationally, it's easy to see that it is impossible to be liked by everyone you encounter. But we humans are not always logical and rational. And it's very human to want to be liked. Nevertheless, to go through life fervently trying not to offend anyone, attempting to gain everyone's approval and affection, will not only fail but it will alienate you from yourself. Currying favor, walking on eggshells, and hoping to be liked by all virtually guarantees a frustrating, phony and empty existence. If you're constantly being who you think others want you to be, you're never really being yourself. Then who are you?

Clearly, if you can choose between being liked or disliked, being liked is better. But if, in order to be liked, you have to seriously compromise your values, ideals, and basic needs, the price will rarely be right. The "yes man" is tolerated by his superiors; he seldom rises to a position of prominence himself.

Although psychological research has pointed out some of the reasons people like one another (e.g., similarity, proximity, shared values), such choices are not always rational. You may never know the reasons. Someone may dislike you simply because you resemble a person who was nasty to her as a child. Your adversary herself may not even know why she dislikes you. You cannot totally avoid the stupidity and prejudice of people who will dislike you for your gender, your race, your appearance, or your sexual orientation.

If someone dislikes you for good reason — because you have injured him, because you have offended, insulted, undermined and inflicted hurt — you can think in terms of reparation, or making amends if possible. But if the other person's antagonism toward you stems from jealousy, prejudice, or some other irrational source, you need to develop a fitting indifference to his or her opinions. It is not irrelevant whether people like you, especially those who are closest to you and those who control goods and services essential to your well-being. But it is self-defeating to "need" the approval of all others.

Your value as a human being doesn't depend on how many people like you!

(Related Toxic Idea: #16 "KEEP YOUR FEELINGS TO YOURSELF.")

Antidotes

Corrective Self-Statements

"My worth as a human being does not depend on anyone's approval."

"It's all right for other people to disapprove of or dislike me or my ideas or actions. What's important is that I don't hurt or exploit others."

"It may even be desirable to be disliked by certain people."

"I will give to others if I enjoy or love them, or if I gain   practical benefits in return. But I will not give to others in order to buy their affection or approval."

"In relationships, quality is more important than quantity."

"Some people may dislike me because of their own 'hangups', not mine."

Positive Counter-Belief

It's important to like yourself
for who and what you are.

Toxic Idea #27

Problems Go Away
If You Ignore Them

Celia and Fred were married for five years and had difficulties from day one. Celia begged Fred to go with her for marriage counseling, but he refused. "I don't want someone else brokering my marriage," he said. One of the biggest drawbacks to problem-solving for this couple was Fred's habit of walking out of the room and refusing to speak to Celia when she raised important issues. (Unfortunately, Fred believed many of the misbeliefs discussed in this book.) He failed to realize that he was shutting all doors to communication by slamming down the phone if Celia called him at work to discuss their problems, and by angrily responding with tirades such as, "I don't want to talk about that!" when they had more time to talk at home after work. Celia finally admitted to herself that Fred wouldn't change, and their marriage ended in an unpleasant divorce.

Analysis

If you leave most distressing issues or problems alone and walk away from them, not only are they likely to continue plaguing you, but they will often get worse. Of course, there is a fine line between a minor problem that is being magnified and is likely to shrink down to size (or disappear) if ignored, and one that requires attention and resolution. Most people have no difficulty making the distinction, but many tend to disregard or gloss over major difficulties that they can ill afford to ignore.

Judd's boss, whom he had known for ten years, suddenly started checking up on his employees. Though he had been somewhat laissez-faire in the past, Kevin was now questioning people about their comings and goings — monitoring private telephone calls, scrutinizing vacation privileges, sick leave, and personal expenses. In his zeal, he made a number of unfounded accusations. Some of his subordinates were becoming increasingly distressed, but Judd advised them simply to ignore the matter. "This is a temporary housecleaning phase," he assured them. "Kevin will grow tired of it in less than two weeks." Judd was correct; things returned to normal in less than two weeks. The minor problem with the boss had almost disappeared.

Almost at the same time, however, a larger problem arose. A new manager had recently joined the firm, a man who was clearly racist and sexist. Jake did not hesitate to voice his prejudices, and those at the receiving end, especially his secretary, became depressed, angry and fearful. Judd could not ignore this matter based on the assumption that it, too, would go away; he took the matter to upper management. After two warnings were ignored, the bigot was fired.

To procrastinate about resolving problems or avoid facing up to disagreeable issues only causes more trouble in the long run. When Celia broached a touchy or painful subject with Fred, and he responded by saying, "I don't want to talk about it!", they shut the doors of communication in their own faces. The problem could only fester. To say "I'd rather talk about it later," is acceptable if the immediate time or place seems inappropriate or uncomfortable, but it doesn't help if this is used as a stalling tactic.

Beware, too, of false positive thinking. It is toxic to sweep problems under the rug by chanting, "Everything will turn out okay," without addressing specific conflicts and solving obvious problems. Most distressing issues or problems, if left alone, do not go away, so don't seal off avenues of hope by ignoring your difficulties or by refusing to talk about them. It's easier in the long run to confront them.

Sometimes it's a good idea to start with those issues that are easiest for you and gradually deal with more difficult matters. For example, here is a list one of our clients drew up: put a new washer on the kitchen faucet; paint the entrance hall; remind Mavis that she still owes me $10; write to Chrysler Motors about the discourteous service manager; see the dentist for the root canal procedure; try to persuade Dad to do something about his drinking.

If at first the problem seems a little overwhelming, don't be too proud or stubborn to seek professional assistance. Chronic avoidance usually means chronic suffering.

Antidotes

Corrective Self-Statements

"*It is better to resolve than to retreat.*"

"*A good faith attempt to deal with problems usually leads to collaboration and greater closeness.*"

"*Only a superficial, deceptive relationship can be pleasant all the time.*"

"*The more I practice confronting important issues, the easier it will become and the more successful I will be at doing it.*"

"*Problems cannot be resolved unless I first acknowledge that they exist.*"

"*To ignore my problems is to ensure that they will persist or get worse.*"

Positive Counter-Belief

Problems don't go away, but most can be solved.

If You Play, Play To Win

If you met Bernie and Denise, husband and wife and both very competitive people, they would tell you up front that for them, winning, getting ahead, and being "number one" are most important. Naturally, they also compete with each other. At a dinner party, for instance, each tries to be the center of attention. They constantly jockey for leadership, and if you saw them playing tennis, you would swear that their lives depended on winning every point. In truth, Bernie and Denise are dissatisfied with life. There are always others who could beat them at their own game, and their extreme envy of those who surpass them causes much misery.

Analysis

Dr. Ronald Goldstein, a psychology professor at Bucks County Community College in Pennsylvania, lectures about "win junkies" — those highly competitive people who are addicted to winning. If such an individual finishes in second place, he thinks he has finished last. For him, the classical pronouncement, "Winning isn't everything, it's the only thing," is most accurate. For such people, the world is divided into winners and losers. Perhaps one of the worst side effects of this mentality is that after winning, they can't afford to sit back and enjoy their accomplishments because they have to keep on winning. People who see everyone else as rivals, who are constantly vying for leadership, miss out on the joys of true collaboration. They create a world of strife, conflict, and cutthroat tactics.

Billy and Joe were buddies in high school and college. Joe dropped out of college while Billy went on to become a successful lawyer. "Joe's a loser," Billy declared. But if you got to know these two men, you would easily see that Joe is a relaxed and happy guy whereas Billy is consumed with ambition and envy.

The "compete and win" philosophy undermines the development of trust in others and precludes the opportunity to benefit from team solutions. Overly competitive people will generally be kept at arm's length. You don't have to be a genius to realize that they don't often inspire your trust. Moreover, it's difficult for others to warm to highly competitive people because they tend to appear hostile or insecure. Those who practice oneupmanship may find that the very people they care about the most are disinclined to be with them.

It's a good feeling when you master a skill or discover you can do certain things really well. You may enjoy competing with yourself while trying to improve certain skills. This is all to the good if you don't overdo it. But lasting happiness rarely results from great achievements and conquests. Instead, it arises from the love and mutual caring that cooperation and close collaboration engender. In fact, there are distinct advantages to being able to participate in certain cooperative ventures. Generally, Paul liked to do projects — especially in biology — by himself. So when his teacher assigned four-person group projects during the unit about the frog, Paul was unhappy. He liked to excel, to get the highest grade working alone. However, he found that he and his three partners worked well as a group, dividing the project into sections as well as working together on the project as a whole. The venture received a high grade, and Paul made three new friends, too.

We urge you to think very carefully about what happens when you pit yourself against another in an attempt to become Number One. Is it wise, in the long run, to gain success by making others fail? Optimum mental and societal well-being demands that our pervasive win/lose attitude be challenged and replaced by a cooperative win-win attitude. Competition has a place in encouraging excellence and improving the quality of products and performance, but it's cooperation which wins the gold medal for *human* values.

Antidotes

Corrective Self-Statements

> *"A focus on winning leads to superficial or distant relationships."*

"Defeating others is probably incompatible with genuine love and friendship."

"The need to win usually stems from insecurity and a desire to impress others."

"Kindness, generosity, warmth, and trust are enduring qualities that engender fondness, not envy and resentment."

"Collaboration is infinitely better than competition."

"Doing things with and for people is usually more self-promoting than achieving goals that undermine others."

Positive Counter-Belief

*If you play, play to enjoy,
to cooperate, to grow.*

Toxic Idea #29

Have Definite Rules For Yourself And Others

Arlene took this toxic misbelief to an extreme. She was fond of saying, "A life without rules is like a ship without a rudder." Her children had to obey more regulations than a recruit in the Marine Corps, and she placed so many demands on herself that she constantly fell short of her own expectations: fulfilling all her obligations to others, always being on time, dressing properly, using correct language, and more. Unlike Kay (Toxic Idea #2), Arlene didn't try to control people; she simply held rather absolutistic views of how things "should be." When people other than her children violated one of her rules (which was often), she typically wouldn't say anything but would feel angry, anxious, guilty, or sad. When the violator was one of her children, punishment was swift and sure.

Analysis

The well-known psychiatrist, Dr. Karen Horney, wrote about "the tyranny of the should," a point that has been extended and amplified by Dr. Albert Ellis, founder of the school of Rational-Emotive Therapy. In essence, the more shoulds, oughts, and musts a person has, the less happy he or she will be. Categorical imperatives — shoulds, oughts, and musts — produce rigid and absolutistic thinking that diminishes the chance for negotiation and compromise. The imposition of shoulds brings defensive and aggressive reactions, not open-minded receptivity.

It is easy to have anger with a "should." How often do you hear people say, "You should have known better than that"? "You shouldn't have made that remark, and I am really furious at you!" And when you "should" on *yourself,* guilt is the net result. "I should have spent more time with my mother!" "I shouldn't have been so up-front with Annie, and now I feel awful!"

If you change shoulds into wishes or preferences, you alter the entire transaction. By removing the shoulds and musts, you stop dumping on yourself and on others, and learning from mistakes becomes easier. "I wish you had done X instead of Y." "I think it would have been better if you had not made that remark." "In retrospect, I wish I'd spent more time with my mother." "It would have been preferable to have been less up front with Annie." This much less-demanding language reduces defensiveness and opens the door to growth.

Try to understand that the more demanding you are — of yourself and others — the less open you become to growth and constructive change. In your daily life, observe what happens when you impose shoulds on others and when they do it to you. Practice stating what you like and dislike rather than imposing your values on others. Catch yourself each time you impose a should, ought, or must on somebody or on yourself (or shouldn'ts and mustn'ts.) We believe you'll find the quality of your relationships tends to improve when you adopt the style we're recommending.

Antidotes

Corrective Self-Statements

> *"Flexibility and moderation are desirable; rigidity and extremism are not."*

> *"We all need principles and guidelines, but not straitjackets."*

> *"The words 'should,' 'ought,' and 'must' are coercive. 'I would like,' 'I would have preferred,' and 'I think it would be better' are much more rational and relationship-enhancing."*

> *"It is far better to state what I like and would desire than to impose shoulds on others or on myself."*

Positive Counter-Belief

Avoid "shoulds" — flexibility increases your chances for happiness.

Toxic Idea #30

Anyone Who Truly Loves You Should Know What You Need

After a whirlwind romance, Martha married Harold because they "seemed to be on the same wavelength and saw eye-to-eye on things." But to her chagrin, as she got to know him better, she realized that he had not "tuned into" some of her finer sensibilities. Perhaps worst of all, she had to tell him how to please her sexually. "If he really loved me," she complained, "he'd know what I need; I shouldn't have to tell him!" She believed that genuine love and true compatibility meant that she could do without words; they would become superfluous in most instances. "If you really care about someone, you should be able to pick up the important things intuitively," she said.

Analysis

When people understand one another and are sensitive to each other's feelings, opinions, and preferences, their relationships are likely to prove rewarding. People who are caring and close often learn to interpret one another's reactions quite accurately. But you cannot expect another person to read your mind. In essence, this is Martha's false belief; "He should know what I want. If I have to spell it out, then our relationship is no good."

On the contrary, deep love and caring do not bestow the powers of telepathy. You cannot experience another person's feelings, regardless of the intensity of your devotion. People, unlike insects, do not possess intricate response patterns based on instinct. Apart from some basic drives (e.g., hunger, thirst) and reflexes (e.g., sucking, swallowing, breathing), whatever people know, they learn through instruction and experience, by example or trial-and-error. In fact, human beings are the only species that *can* communicate complex thoughts and feelings through spoken language. In relationships with each other, then, they get along best when they communicate those thoughts and feelings clearly!

One of the most harmful features of this toxic idea is that it can lead people to fall into self-defeating traps. Here's an example: "If Johnny truly loves me," claims Diane, "he'll offer to drive me over to see Aunt Celia when she comes home from her trip." According to Diane's line of reasoning, if Johnny fails the test, he "proves" he doesn't really care. How much better it would be for Diane not to play games but to state her request in a straightforward way: "Will you do me a favor and drive me over to Aunt Celia's house?"

This telepathic expectation is evident in a verbatim dialogue one of us recently had with a 40-year-old patient who has been complaining that her husband has stopped loving her.

Therapist: *Has Bill said he no longer loves you?*

Patient: *Not in so many words, but I can tell.*

Therapist: *How can you tell? Is he acting differently?*

Patient: *I have a perfect example. When we were getting ready for work this morning, Bill offered to drive our cat to the vet. When I said it wasn't necessary, he pushed off, leaving me to make all the arrangements about the cat.*

Therapist: *What does that prove? Hadn't you declined his offer? Didn't you say that it...*

Patient: *So what! I really wanted him to help me out. If he loved me, he'd have known that.*

The same telepathic expectations are evident in Joan and Frank's relationship. When Joan asked her husband if she should invite certain friends over for dinner, he declared, "I'm not in the mood for them or anyone else." Later, when he found out that she had made no dinner arrangements, he said, "If you really loved me, you would have realized that I was merely expressing a temporary feeling."

Rich, fulfilling relationships are based on your willingness to clearly and openly communicate your basic needs, loves, hates and desires. *You* need to teach people how best to get along with you. Say what you mean, mean what you say, and do not expect anyone to read your mind.

Antidotes

Corrective Self-Statements

"People who set psychological traps are the ones who usually fall into them."

"No one can be completely tuned into another person's thoughts and feelings."

"I need to state clearly what I want and how I feel; I cannot expect anyone to read my mind."

"No matter how much people love and care for me, they can still misread or misunderstand me."

"Open, honest and direct statements of your desires and hopes are the best means of achieving loving communication."

"Setting traps in order to test people's love and loyalty show of hostility."

Positive Counter-Belief

State your wishes and desires
openly and clearly;
anyone who really loves you
deserves no less.

Insults Are Bound To Be Upsetting

Sarah was described as "very touchy." She was quick to take offense, to feel hurt by people's remarks, and to become angry and depressed if she felt that someone had belittled her. Her younger sister commented: "You have to watch your P's and Q's around Sarah. She's so thin-skinned that she gets bruised by the slightest comments."

Analysis

It is difficult not to be sensitive to criticism, rejection, and disapproval. If someone "bad-mouths" you, you're hurt, perhaps devastated, as Sarah so often is. Though as children you probably learned the old adage, "Sticks and stones may break my bones but words can never hurt me," you most likely don't fully accept or believe this idea because you're human, and sometimes other people *do* hurt you with insults.

But the idea that insults are *inevitably* upsetting is mistaken; it contends that it is virtually *impossible* for you to avoid getting upset over insulting remarks and put-downs, that you need exceptional strength to remain calm and indifferent under attack. In fact, some people even say that they would *prefer* to get upset about offensive comments or statements instead of remaining untouched and indifferent. "Why let another person get away with insults?" they ask.

The point is that in nearly every situation you *can* avoid becoming emotionally distraught when you feel you've been insulted. Refined, caring, sensitive, and informed people are not likely to hurl insults. So when you are at the receiving end of verbal abuse, the first thing to realize is that the speaker's own conflict or problem probably ignited the attack, not you or something you said or did. After all, an intelligent, self-confident person has no need to ridicule you or put you down.

Instead of upsetting yourself over callous or insulting remarks, try to develop an attitude of curiosity about the speaker by asking yourself, "What's going on with this person?" Thus, when Myra's husband, Fred, said to her, "You are a pygmy brain, and your mother is a numbskull!"

Myra did not sulk or go on the offensive. Instead, she asked Fred, "What's really bothering you?" and was able to get to the heart of the matter.

Unfortunately, some people, like enemies in old Westerns, require a duel to the death for the slightest insult. But you can avoid such extreme responses. You're often better off ignoring putdowns and insults, not dignifying them with a response. Letting them upset you means that you are giving the speaker, whose problem it was in the first place, undue power.

Whenever possible, avoid people who make it a habit to be verbally abusive or offensive. If responding to an insult seems worth your time and energy, answer assertively to show the offender your displeasure, as Myra did with Fred. Or, use irony and humor, which in some situations can diffuse the tension of a verbal attack. For instance, when Joan tried to upset Olga by referring to her as "a little farm girl," Olga simply smiled and said, "I guess that's why I prefer pigs, mules, goats and cows to certain people." In some situations, because the remarks address specific issues without ridicule, the negative comments might be helpful to you even if you don't like the other person. For example, when Harry turned to Bud and said, "Your suit makes you look like you're off to a funeral," Bud simply replied, "I guess this coat and tie do look a bit somber." In all cases, the key is to avoid becoming emotionally distraught when you're on the receiving end of insults from anyone.

(Related Toxic Ideas: #2 "YOU'RE BETTER OFF WHEN YOU CONTROL OTHER PEOPLE" and #22 "CRITICISM IS A GOOD WAY TO CORRECT PEOPLE'S MISTAKES.")

Antidotes

Corrective Self-Statements

> *"It's healthy to be a little thick-skinned at times and not take others' negative styles personally."*

> *"I can ignore putdowns and insults if I choose to."*

> *"Those who are abusive and insulting often have something seriously wrong with them."*

> *"When someone loses her cool, try to be curious and ask, 'What's really bothering this person?'"*

> *"You do not have to give undue power to other people's remarks."*

Positive Counter-Belief

Insults don't hurt unless you let them.

Being Hard On Yourself
Is Good For You

Keith was a pretty fair and tolerant guy, except when it came to himself. His standards for others were different from those he set for himself. "I'm very hard on myself," he would say. In fact, he treated himself abominably. When he failed to meet his self-imposed sales goals, for instance, he came down on himself like the proverbial "ton of bricks." While he displayed democratic tolerance toward others, he showed a fascistic intolerance when it came to any real or imagined shortcoming in himself. His attitude seemed to result from an overly strict upbringing and a feeling of being superior to others ("I can do better...”). Thus, standards acceptable for his co-workers, his family or his friends were not nearly high enough for him.

Analysis

This toxic belief overlaps to some extent with #7 (PERFECTION SHOULD BE YOUR GOAL) and #25 (WE ALL DO OUR BEST WHEN WE HAVE HIGH EXPECTATIONS), but here we are addressing individuals, like Keith, who have a clear-cut double standard, those who tend to be very easy on others but are extremely hard on themselves. "I'd never treat anyone else the way I treat myself," one woman remarked. Her problem turned out to be one of undue self-hatred, for which she required intensive therapy. But less extreme cases abound — individuals who would be horrified to witness unkind acts to others, but see nothing wrong in being mean and nasty to themselves. They are unaware that most people who deplore acts of intolerance, impatience, criticism, condemnation, unfairness, or prejudice tend to react the same way whether they observe these negative attitudes in others or in themselves. "I don't like to see anyone being treated harshly," one man remarked, "and it makes no difference if I see you dishing out unfair treatment to others or to yourself."

We typically ask our patients who engage in self-flagellation to carefully note putdowns of themselves for a week or two. "That will give you a pretty good idea of what you're doing to yourself," we tell them. But some extremely self-deprecating people carry their notebooks around for weeks and write nothing in them. They are so used to their negative self-descriptions, they are unaware of the statements they're making and see nothing unusual about them.

The patients who put themselves down tell us that they hadn't noticed any negative statements in the previous week or two. Typically, within the next thirty minutes, we will tune into more than a dozen putdowns. When we call their attention to some of them, we are often told, "Those are not negative statements; they're just reality." Perfectionists are apt to fall into this trap more often than most people (see Toxic Idea #7). They call themselves "stupid" because they cannot reach some incredible standard they've set for themselves; they call themselves "fat" or "ugly" because they don't look like professional models.

Try to become aware of the times you put yourself down. Carry a small notebook in your pocket or purse and jot down all instances of negative self-talk as soon as possible. Become aware of the messages you send to yourself. Do you catch yourself making self-deprecating generalizations such as, "I sound like a complete fool!", "I fail at everything I do!", "I'm an idiot!", or "I don't deserve good things!"?

Negative, self-critical putdowns will usually result in negative emotions and unfortunate results. If you are consistently hard on yourself, you need to lighten up, to realize that everyone is fallible, and to work hard at becoming self-tolerant and self-accepting. This does not mean that a self-indulgent lifestyle is advantageous and should be cultivated. Avoid extremes. But if you are very hard on yourself, if you often demean and devalue yourself, you're likely to be needlessly unhappy. Instead, remind yourself of the opening line of an ancient Hebraic philosophy, which states: "If I am not for myself, who will be for me?"

Antidotes
Corrective Self-Statements

"I can be tolerant of myself and others."

"I have certain limitations that I need to accept, not deplore."

"It's okay to expect more from myself, but excessive demands usually result in unhappiness and a poor self-concept."

"Self-criticism and self-downing diminish self-esteem; self-acceptance and self-tolerance improve self-esteem."

"Being hard on myself is only okay if it leads to constructive change and greater self-acceptance."

"Self-affirmation will get me further in life than self-condemnation."

Positive Counter-Belief

Treat yourself and others fairly.

Toxic Idea #33

An Apology Wipes The Slate Clean

Seth insisted that his children should apologize after behaving badly. "Say you're sorry," he said after his 8-year-old son had punched a neighbor's 5-year-old daughter in the abdomen. Seth told his son to go over to the neighbors and apologize. He was extremely angry when the neighbors stated that simply saying, "I'm sorry," was insufficient. "What more do you expect the kid to do?" Seth asked.

Analysis

It is intriguing how many people exclaim, "You owe me an apology!" and become inordinately upset when someone refuses to utter the two magic words — "I'm sorry." Certainly, there is value in apologizing for offensive behavior and in trying to make amends with those "magic words." But for many, it is a simple matter to say "I'm sorry" over and over again without meaning it and without changing their actions. Seth didn't recognize the need to teach his son this lesson — to make amends by *actions* as well as *words*.

Dee has not learned this lesson either. She refused to speak to her sister, Jane, until Jane apologized for an inappropriate remark she had made about Dee. Finally, when Jane told Dee that she was sorry, Dee was satisfied. She got what she wanted — the verbal apology — but it was obvious to everyone else that Jane did not mean it.

Many people like Jane and Dee believe that apologies should be automatically accepted and that as long as someone has asked to be pardoned, all should be forgiven. They're dismayed when someone says, in effect, "Apologizing is a good beginning, but what are you going to *do* about it — now and in the future?" Too many people seem to believe that they can behave abominably as long as they're willing to apologize afterwards. They don't see that the important thing is to refrain from repeating the same mistake in the future. One individual who had embezzled money from a friend actually remarked, "Well, I *said* I was sorry!"

Words are simply words: "I'm terribly sorry!" "Please forgive me!" "I was wrong!" "I beg your pardon!" If the person saying these words is genuine and sincere, the apology, depending on the wrongdoing, may suffice. But unscrupulous people can wring their hands in phony agony, express profound regret, and mean none of it. When truly assertive people feel they have been mistreated, they are seldom concerned about extracting an apology (especially an empty one). They simply state in a firm and forthright manner how they feel and *what they want changed from that point on*: "What can you or I do to be sure this doesn't happen again?"

(Related Toxic Idea: #11 "INCONSIDERATE RELATIVES OR FRIENDS DESERVE THE SILENT TREATMENT.")

Antidotes

Corrective Self-Statements

> *"Empty apologies are of no value."*

> *"An apology might help to explain a misdeed, but won't undo its damage."*

> *"Apologies are helpful only if they're sincere."*

> *"It's easy to let someone say 'I'm sorry'. But asking someone to correct a misdeed is what's important."*

> *"Apologies have merit only if people are willing to change their actions."*

Positive Counter-Belief

> *Apologies are words;*
> *corrective actions count more.*

Toxic Idea #34

To Change, You Must Understand The Reasons For Your Behavior

Beatrice, a 56-year-old author, had seen psychiatrists and psychologists on and off for 50 years. At the age of six, when she was underachieving at school, her parents took her to a counselor. At ten she was in therapy with a psychiatrist, upset over her parents' divorce. As a teenager, she saw a therapist for a mild eating disorder. In her early twenties she sought psychotherapy after a broken romance. Later, she underwent nine years of psychoanalysis because she was often depressed about her career. Although being in therapy had been a way of life for her, Beatrice's overriding belief was that she still lacked certain insights. That's the reason, she concluded, that she worried too much, demanded too much from herself, often felt depressed or became too easily upset, and remained less self-confident than she desired. She believed that if only she understood herself more fully, she would be much better off.

Analysis

There is certainly no direct relationship between insight and action or between self-understanding and emotional control. Many people can be profoundly aware of the reasons for their feelings and actions and still not change, no matter how highly motivated, as Beatrice's history shows. Conversely, people willing to work hard have successfully changed their negative behavior without ever exploring its origins. Tens of thousands of college students, for example, have overcome anxiety about exams through straightforward behavioral treatments involving no inquiry into the past.

The process of understanding yourself and changing your behavior is not an either/or proposition. Understanding yourself often proves helpful, but while you explore the reasons behind your feelings and actions, you need to change the negative behavior.

If some of your habits, feelings, or notions undermine your happiness, you are more likely to overcome them by resolving to *do* something different here and now rather than by dwelling on what went wrong then and there. Understanding why you are the way you are will not necessarily enable you to change. *Doing* is what counts. Joann acquired deep and profound insights in analysis, but was nevertheless unable to change her self-defeating habit of avoiding social situations until she learned new ways of being at ease with groups of people through assertiveness training. Knowing *what to do* about a problem is often more helpful than understanding *why* or *how* it arose.

Antidotes

Corrective Self-Statements

"Focusing on the change in behavior in the present and future often leads to more psychological growth than dwelling on the past."

"It is better to change how you act and think than merely to explore your thoughts and actions."

"Psychological change and personal growth are more likely to result from corrective action than from self-understanding."

"Insight alone, no matter how profound, is seldom necessary or sufficient for psychological change."

"Figuring out why something happens or happened is usually less important than discovering what to do about it."

"The best insights usually involve discovering and changing psychologically unhealthy thinking (toxic ideas)."

Positive Counter-Belief

To change your life,
do something in the present;
don't wait until you understand the past.

Cover Your Mistakes;
The Important Thing Is To Be Right

Victor is a retired machinist whose concern for precision and accuracy went far beyond his successful career. He was convinced that anyone who is shown to be wrong looks like a fool. It didn't matter to him if the error were an inaccurate measurement, a mistaken view, a faulty conclusion, or an invalid opinion. "You mustn't lose face," was one of his favorite sayings. Humans are not like machines, of course, and Victor sometimes tried to "save face" in social situations by acting as if he were right (even when he knew he was wrong). He failed to realize that many people disliked his air of certainty even on matters about which he knew very little, and that he lost their affection and respect for behaving this way.

Analysis

We all like to be right. There is a particular human pleasure that comes from drawing correct conclusions.

When the teacher says "That's right!" the student feels proud and pleased. Conversely, the judgement, "That's wrong; you failed the exam," can lead to a fear of making errors, and as a result, more errors.

Most of us recognize that in the realm of human activities, few things are 100% right or wrong. Yet all our social systems offer positive reinforcement for being "right" — in school, on the job, in politics, in sports. As a result, many people grow up on guard, covering up their mistakes.

Gordon was a medical intern who was told to obtain blood samples and urine specimens from four patients. When he forgot to ask the patients for urine samples, he made up false reports rather than admit his error. One of the nurses found out and reported him to the chief physician. Gordon was suspended from the hospital, and the medical board received formal notification of his infraction. Had he simply admitted his error, he would have received only a reprimand for his forgetfulness.

Others fail to take action at all for fear of making a mistake, of being proved wrong. They become tense and defensive. John actively participated in class discussions and wrote insightful papers in high school English classes. When he got to college, however, he became almost paralyzed — virtually unable to speak or write — in his first English class for fear of being proven wrong by better-prepared classmates.

Adopting an "I-am-right/You-are-wrong" position is unwise. You may win many battles this way, as the saying goes, but you'll end up losing the war. Some people not only insist on being right at all times, but when they win an argument, they gloat and boast about it. People who behave this way are typically called "insufferable," and — like

Victor in the example above — they and their know-it-all responses typically alienate other people.

They don't realize that they'd be wiser to be wrong and acknowledge it than to be right and boast about it. If an "insufferable" person puts you down for making a mistake, you need to realize that there is probably something wrong with *him* or *her*. (See Toxic Misbelief #16.) In fact, others usually shun those who so adamantly need to be right and so constantly try to prove that they're right.

We have seen many marriages falter because certain husbands and wives insist on "being right." Indeed, when they can prove that their partners were wrong about something, they tend to rub it in. This behavior hardly promotes love and closeness. Instead, it creates a competitive and defensive atmosphere and distance that can eventually tear a couple apart.

The key is to realize that everyone is fallible, everyone makes mistakes, and everyone is wrong from time to time. When you make mistakes, don't cover them up in order to appear to be right. In fact, it is often actually helpful to draw attention to errors you have made. This action not only enables you to learn from your mistakes, but other people see you as more human, and you gain their trust.

Maud, a legal secretary, was asked to type up a brief from one of the partners' handwritten notes. By mistake, she left out a page. Upon discovering her error, she apologized to the partner and asked for the handwritten copies in order to append the missing page and retype any others. Her error did result in two hours of overtime and some embarrassment, but her boss met the client on time with the full manuscript the next morning.

Think about the possible consequences for Maud, the

attorney, and the client had she tried to cover up her mistake!

These honest admissions, "I'm sorry," "I don't know," and "I was wrong," far from making you appear foolish, inspire others to trust and respect you. Denying or covering up mistakes prevent personal growth; admitting and learning from mistakes promote it.

Antidotes

Corrective Self-Statements

"It's usually not wise to pretend to know something that you really don't know."

"Everyone makes mistakes; the important thing is learning from them."

"Mistakes are opportunities for personal growth, not signs of stupidity or weakness."

"Being right and coming across as a know-it-all usually discourages friendship and intimacy."

"Covering up errors and pretending to know it all reveals insecurity and prevents learning."

"It is much better to be happy than to be right."

Positive Counter-Belief

Nobody's perfect;
take credit when you're right;
admit when you're not

Toxic Idea #36

You Won't Go Wrong If You Follow Your Gut Feelings

Erika always trusted her gut feelings. When Len, one of her friends and co-workers, passed her in the hall without greeting her, she felt hurt and angry because her gut told her that he would have said "hello" if he really liked her. Thus, deep down, she knew that Len probably disliked her and was not interested in her. Why else would he have behaved as he did? What had she done to deserve such treatment? Because she trusted her feelings, Erika concluded that Len was a jerk and decided to have nothing to do with him. Later that morning when he asked her out to lunch, Erika told him to "find someone else to eat with," and walked away in a huff.

Analysis

Human beings have the most highly developed capacities for rational thought and reason of all living creatures. Nevertheless, many people, like Erika, too often trust their emotional reactions and gut feelings rather than reason when faced with ambiguous situations. While your gut reactions are sometimes accurate, often they are not. When you exclusively trust your feelings on such occasions, unnecessary conflict, needless errors, and misunderstandings often result.

Clyde, one of our clients got into serious financial difficulties because he trusted his gut feelings and his intuition. When he was offered the opportunity to buy beach front property, he emptied his savings account to do so. "My gut told me that this was a good investment," he said. Soon, because the property market virtually collapsed, he lost all the money he had invested. Had he consulted knowledgeable investors to ask for their opinions instead of following his own instincts, he would probably have been warned that this deal was too risky.

You reason with your brain, not with your gut. Let your reason prevail over your emotional reactions. Before allowing a feeling to become a belief, look for rational *evidence* that can support your feeling. Too many people engage in circular reasoning. For example, Susan reasoned that when Bill seemed to avoid talking to her at a party, he had deliberately intended to make her mad.

Evidence to support or refute an idea can come from two main sources — agreement from others whose opinions you respect, and your own actual experience. Thus, if Erika had asked several other respected co-workers if Len was mad at her, she would have had some evidence either to confirm or contradict her feelings. Or, if she had checked her perceptions with Len directly, she would have had even more accurate evidence either to support or refute her gut feelings.

Before automatically equating your gut feelings with truth, seek some evidence to confirm or refute their accuracy. In essence, dig for facts before jumping to conclusions. (See Toxic Idea #17: "FIRST IMPRESSIONS ARE BEST.")

Antidotes

Corrective Self-Statements

"The thought or feeling is not the same as the fact."

"Just because I think it or feel strongly about something doesn't automatically mean it's true."

"Seeking facts is better than jumping to conclusions."

"Try to let rational thought prevail over emotional reactions."

"We can trust our gut reactions up to a point, but it is best to double-check the facts."

"It is unwise to make important decisions on gut reactions alone."

"When in doubt, remember that your brain is in your head, not in your gut."

Positive Counter-Belief

Gut feelings can be wrong;
seek solid evidence before you act.

Toxic Idea #37

Life Should Be Fair

Morris was honest, decent, and hardworking. He had been raised to believe that people like him — who care about others, work hard, have integrity, pray to God, treat others fairly, abhor violence, donate money to charity, do not gossip, behave well, read widely and well, are opposed to prejudice and discrimination, and go out of their way not to judge others — will receive their just rewards. Such people, he had been taught, will be successful and happy and get ahead in life. Morris's boss, Simon, was ill-tempered, nasty, dishonest, rude, manipulative, and uncaring, and it was Simon who seemed to reap major dividends and enjoy the richest spoils. "Life's so unfair!" exclaimed Morris.

Analysis

How wonderful if it were possible to live in a world where hatred, bigotry, violence and exploitation were unknown; where people were incapable of rape, robbery, murder, unprovoked assault, or dishonesty; where the fairness Morris longed for was evident everywhere. But in our real world — where events and circumstances are often so arbitrary — good things often happen to people like Simon, and dreadful things commonly befall good, kind, decent, gentle, and loving ones. In short, life is anything but fair. In fact, many of the things that happen are decidedly, and sometimes profoundly, unfair.

There is some evidence that immoral people, no matter how much fame, wealth, or power they obtain, cannot experience the true inner happiness that honest people enjoy. This phenomenon might seem fairer were it always true, but all too often it is the despicable individuals who receive the best of everything — including good health — while truly noble souls may suffer miserably.

There are many, of course, who find solace in the belief that evil and wicked people will be punished in the hereafter. Maybe yes, maybe no.

Those who fully grasp the reality of the inherent unfairness of life do not waste time lamenting, complaining, and crying over unfair treatment. They don't withdraw into romance novels or television soaps; they don't seek solace in alcohol or other mind-altering drugs; they don't retreat to purely intellecutal contemplation of the meaning of life. Instead, they adopt a healthy and realistic resolve to get on with life, to make the best of it and live it to the fullest. These hardy souls try to *do* something about the unfairness insofar as they can influence or change the circumstances.

When unfair events or circumstances occur, these people strive mightily to correct the unfairness in some way.

John Callahan, the famous cartoonist, became quadriplegic following an auto accident, and no one could have blamed him for spending his life as a self-pitying, nonfunctioning person. But, after struggling with alcoholism for several years, he started using the one hand that he could barely move to draw brilliant, hillarious and scathing cartoons about disabilities. He has achieved enormous success and has served as an inspiration to people all over the world who are similarly afflicted.

We can't all deal with the consequences of life's unfairness in exactly the same way or necessarily with the same degree of success, but to live a productive life and to adopt an attitude of acceptance are far better than complaining or withdrawing.

You can live out this philosophy in raising your children to view life from the same realistic perspective, by not teaching them to believe that justice and mercy will triumph, that good will always win over evil, and that life is fair. Instead, develop and encourage in them a sense of fair-play, integrity, decency, kindness, loyalty, and compassion.

Whenever you are commiserating about the unfairness you've experienced, ask yourself, "What am I doing about it?" A change will be necessary, either in what you do about the situation or in how you view it — or both.

Antidotes

Corrective Self-Statements

"Total fairness and happy endings occur often in fairy tales, only occasionally in real life."

"It's bad enough that life is often unfair. Why make things worse by insisting upon the impossibility of complete fairness?"

"Unfairness is inevitable; misery about it is optional."

"It's sensible to desire fair treatment, but to demand it usually ends in frustration and despair."

"The fact that I prefer fairness does not mean that misery inevitably has to follow every unfair event in my life."

"I don't have to like the fact that life is often unfair, nor do I have to be bitter and discouraged by it."

Positive Counter-Belief

Life is not fair,
but you can take action to make it better.

Toxic Idea #38

Happily Married People Don't Have Sexual Feelings For Anyone Else

Claire was extremely upset. Married a little more than two years, she and her husband were at a party where she danced with John, a charming and attractive single man. To her chagrin, Claire found herself "anything but repulsed" when John gave her a friendly kiss. "I love my husband very deeply," she declared. "We have so much in common, our sex life is great, and I am completely satisfied by him." Her reaction at the party led her to doubt her own feelings and the strength of her marriage. She was sure that her mother had never entertained even a fleeting sexual thought or feeling for anyone but her father. The simple fact that she had noticed how sexy and attractive John had been led her to question the viability of her marriage. She believed that the title of a very old song — "I Only Have Eyes For You" — genuinely reflected the feelings of people who are truly in love.

Analysis

Several species of birds and other animals are instinctively monogamous and mate for life, unable to survive without one another. While some people may find such devotion appealing, no such code of complete exclusivity is written into our DNA. Men and women, no matter how happily married, are capable of noticing, thinking about, and responding to the physical and sexual attractiveness of many others.

In fact, human beings are capable of being aroused and excited by thousands of different individuals. A vast number of people, for example, are excited by watching their favorite film stars. They can enjoy erotic fantasies without undermining their own marriages.

A related myth is the romantic notion that there is one special person out there — Mr. or Ms. Right — and when you meet this preordained individual, lifelong bliss will follow. In such a union, the couple is supposed to be so intensely and deeply devoted to each other that they remain oblivious to others, without the slightest awareness of someone else's charms. If you doubt that people in this day and age entertain such absurd notions, we wish you could meet some of the people who ask us to help them overcome jealousy and insecurity.

"Is there something wrong with me?" Sandra inquired. "When I see a sexy guy, I undress him mentally and wonder what he'd be like in bed." (You didn't believe that this behavior was an exclusively male prerogative, did you?) Sandra was told that if she acted out her fantasies, she would likely suffer major consequences: damage to her primary relationship and high risk of acquiring a sexually transmitted disease. "Lord no!" she said, "I'd never go further than thinking about it. I have no wish to cheat on my boyfriend." "Then enjoy yourself," her counselor advised.

Sandra's experience and behavior were perfectly normal; people do not have to act on their fantasies, but most of us have them and enjoy them, even in the best of marriages or committed relationships. (Those who do not have such fantasies are certainly not abnormal, however!)

Antidotes
Corrective Self-Statements

> *"It's natural to experience sexual feelings for many people."*

> *"We can't always choose to whom we are attracted or when."*

> *"We can more easily control our actions than our feelings."*

> *"It's possible and normal to have sexual feelings for many people in addition to my partner."*

> *"It can spice up my sex life to fantasize about different sexual scenarios."*

Positive Counter-Belief

It is quite normal to experience
sexual attraction for others;
to act on such feelings can have
serious negative consequences.

Your Word Is Your Bond; Never Break A Promise

Leon developed food poisoning and was up all night vomiting and suffering from chills and stomach pains. The next day he was a little better but still felt dreadful. Nevertheless, by 8:30 a.m. he arrived at his friend Jake's house ready to help move furniture from a U-Haul into Jake's new place. Within half an hour, Leon collapsed and ended up in the emergency room of the local hospital with a high fever and a dangerous level of dehydration. It took him a week to recuperate. When asked why he had not called Jake to explain that he had been too ill to help move furniture, Leon said, "I had given him my word that come hell or high water I'd be there the next morning."

Analysis

People admire and respect someone who keeps promises and whose word really means something. "You can depend on Charles. If he promises to do something, you can count on it." But if Charles is willing to endanger himself, as Leon did, rather than go back on his word, his judgement is in serious doubt. In fact, Leon's actions show such extreme rigidity, you would be right to question not only his judgement, but also his intelligence.

Perhaps you doubt that anyone would be as rigid and perhaps as stupid as Leon, but we have seen evidence of this type of rigidity while working with many different individuals. Nick even went through with his marriage ceremony despite serious misgivings because, he said, "I had given my word."

When a child says, "No matter what happens, promise to take me to the zoo on Sunday," the wise adult never agrees to such unconditional terms. A sensible credo is to do your utmost to keep a promise unless extenuating circumstances interfere with your ability to do so. Indeed, you need to teach children, as early as possible, (and adults need to realize) that in the real world unconditional promises are unrealistic, unwise, and unacceptable. Thus, even if you have promised your children that "no matter what happens, we will go to the zoo tomorrow," they must understand that you are entitled to break your promise if you develop food poisoning or fracture a leg!

Before making a promise, think very carefully about what you're agreeing to do or guaranteeing not to do. Instead of unwisely saying, "No matter what happens, I promise faithfully to do XYZ," state your promises straightforwardly and realistically: "I give my word, my solemn promise that I will do XYZ *unless* A or B or C prevents me from doing so."

Antidotes
Corrective Self-Statements

> *"Don't make or take promises lightly, but remember that sometimes unavoidable or unexpected circumstances may force you to break them."*

> *"It is foolish to make unconditional promises."*

> *"It's best to keep your word unless doing so is dangerous or foolish."*

> *"It's important to be understanding and nonjudgmental if someone breaks a promise for a valid reason."*

> *"Remember that someone who only breaks promises 5 or 10% of the time is 90-95% trustworthy."*

Positive Counter-Belief

Keep your word unless serious and unanticipated circumstances prevent it.

Suffering And Hard Work Build Character

Hank and Betty came from poor families and struggled for many years to make ends meet. Hank had been abandoned at birth and was raised by abusive foster parents. Betty was one of six children and had to drop out of school to help support her younger siblings. The couple were now very well off financially, but their two children were raised according to the principle, "no pain, no gain." In order for Hank and Betty's children to get parental love and approval, they had to get straight A's in school and hold jobs as well. Their parents saw to it that they were not spoiled, had "good" values, were imbued with the work ethic, and realized that "you don't get something for nothing." Although Hank and Betty could have made life a lot easier for their children, they wanted them to have the high self-esteem that they felt came only from sacrifice.

Analysis

Do you believe that suffering is really necessary to achieve the good life? Look at your own life and that of anyone you know who is motivated by this unrelenting attitude toward to see if you think it has brought happiness. While hard work is sometimes a passion, few people benefit from suffering. Life is difficult enough without assuming that adversity is good. Have we learned nothing from Dickens?

Many despicable, bitter, selfish people have suffered and sacrificed all their lives. Many warm, kind, considerate and generous people have not experienced much adversity or ever worked unusually hard. While individuals often do learn, grow, and gain perspective from hardship, suffering is neither necessary nor desirable to build character.

Hank and Betty are right about one thing: it is important not to spoil children by offering them anything they want regardless of how they act. Although hard work won't necessarily build character, it can help children learn responsibility, integrity, fairness, and the skills for achieving their potential. Happy, healthy children (and adults) discover that work can bring tangible rewards, and the sense of autonomy that comes with knowing you're not dependent upon others or society. But to demand hard work or suffering solely in the name of "building character" may instead build resentment, resistance, and callouses.

What does build good character is having exemplary role models (e.g., parents, friends, teachers, neighbors, doctors, school bus drivers) who reinforce desirable qualities and constructively correct less desirable behavior.

A person of "good character" is ethical, responsible, compassionate, reliable, sincere, honest, dependable, socially aware, generous, charitable, tolerant, forgiving, and trustworthy. In what ways does adversity build these character traits? It doesn't! In fact, people who suffer undue or unnecessary hardship are more likely to become bitter. One of our colleagues who has worked in the criminal justice system for many years told us that he has encountered numerous lawbreakers who justified their actions by claiming that life had been very tough for them and that they were therefore entitled to rob, rape, or even to kill.

A clear-cut example of a case in which sacrifice failed to build character or to "pay off" in any way, comes from Julian, a 30-year-old accountant. He carried the hard-work-is-good-for-you philosophy to extremes, and in addition to his full-time job, he moonlighted. During the income tax season, he boasted about spending at least 18 hours at work each day. Working long hours made him feel especially virtuous, and he bragged that he probably made more money than any other accountant of his age in the country.

On one rare break from his work schedule, Julian accepted an invitation to join his family at a picnic. Several young people were present — friends of his sister and older brother — and he heard one of them remark, "Julian seems to have just flown in from Mars." Julian had not seen a movie in years; he knew nothing about the theater, sporting events, television or current events. He had not dated since graduating from college, but he could wax eloquent about tax laws, tax shelters, and investments, including stocks, bonds, real estate and more.

The crowning blow for Julian came when he was fired from his job for embezzling funds. He justified his deed by claiming that he had worked harder than anyone else at the firm and was entitled to extra compensation. Hard work had not done much to build Julian's character!

While Julian's case, once again, is rather extreme, it underscores the point that we have made throughout the book: aim for balance, avoid mutually exclusive, either/or thinking, and try to sidestep excesses of any kind.

Antidotes

Corrective Self-Statements

"Adversity will find you often enough; it's foolish to seek it out on purpose."

"Life is hard enough as it is. Why make it any harder?"

"People who suffer don't necessarily have better characters than those who experience fun and enjoyment."

"Suffering and adversity may help you develop good coping skills, but won't necessarily foster decency and honesty."

"There is little to be gained by needless self-sacrifice and hardship."

Positive Counter-Belief

Good role models and sensitivity to others build character.

Afterword

The forty toxic ideas that comprise this book represent those we have seen most frequently in our practices over the past several years. This book provides a ready and handy reference that can be easily carried around for quick reminders when necessary.

There are, of course, some additional myths we frequently encounter in our work, including many that were "close contenders" for inclusion in *Don't Believe It for a Minute!* Some have been addressed in our other books (e.g., *I Can If I Want To*, by A. Lazarus & Fay; *PQR: Prescription for a Quality Relationship* by Fay; *Marital Myths: Two Dozen Mistaken Beliefs that Can Ruin a Marriage or Make a Bad One Worse* by A. Lazarus.) Twenty-three close contenders are listed below. See if you can thoroughly dispute and provide antidotes for each of these misbeliefs.

* Getting married will make you happy.
* Show other people that you know more than they do.
* Having money inevitably brings joy and pleasure into people's lives.
* Fame brings happiness.

* Having children brings fulfillment and joy.
* You should always think positive, kind and loving thoughts.
* Do what is expected of you.
* Listen to the experts — they always know best.
* To get anywhere in life, you must have definite goals.
* You can believe the printed word.
* Once you start something you should always finish it.
* The more you pay for something the better it is.
* You are totally responsible for your life and for everything that happens to you.
* You are not responsible for your life or anything that happens to you.
* People are basically altruistic.
* What happens to you is controlled entirely by fate.
* Changing your mind is a sign of weakness.
* Great sex is not possible without deep love and devotion.
* Emotional displays are a sign of weakness.
* If you don't feel like doing something, don't do it.
* You first need to feel confident before tackling a difficult task.
* If something is uncomfortable, avoid it.
* You need to be fully in control of yourself at all times.

The list of toxic ideas with which we all afflict ourselves is almost endless. It is in fact a worthwhile goal to develop a "sixth sense" about the noxious and toxic misbeliefs that surround us and inevitably have an unfortunate impact upon us, and to dispel them as soon as possible. The fewer you embrace, the better your life will be. There is a distinct "ripple effect" that occurs with the work you do on such misbeliefs. The process of working on some of them makes it easier to recognize and conquer others. When you effectively dispute one, it gives you both the courage and the method to apply to others.

As we noted in the Introduction, misbeliefs are like faulty road maps. If you follow them you can become hopelessly lost and bewildered. To stay on the right course, you need to correct your maps. It is also important that the vehicle you are driving be in good repair as well. Some personal unhappiness and faulty thinking are at least partially a result of biological disorders such as severe depression, schizophrenia and some body image disturbances. For the successful resolution of these problems, prescribed medications may be necessary, in addition to the challenging of irrational beliefs. If consistent and diligent application of the methods we recommend does not lead to your feeling better, consultation with a professional therapist may be indicated.

We all need to take charge of our toxic misbeliefs, and to replace them with reasoned facts, or they will surely poison our lives. It is difficult to love and be loved in the face of faulty thinking or mistaken ideas. If you are willing to work at identifying and changing the erroneous notions you may endorse, the quality of your life is bound to improve.

MORE BOOKS WITH *IMPACT*

We think you will find these Impact Publishers titles of interest:

MARITAL MYTHS: Two Dozen Mistaken Beliefs That Can Ruin A Marriage (Or Make A Bad One Worse)
Arnold Allan Lazarus, Ph.D.
Softcover: $7.95 1985 176pp
Famed psychologist/marriage therapist examines false ideas which lead couples astray.

ACCEPTING EACH OTHER: Individuality and Intimacy in Your Loving Relationship
Michael L. Emmons, Ph.D. and Robert E. Alberti, Ph.D.
Softcover: $9.95   1991   240pp
Enrich your loving partnership by developing six key dimensions: attraction, communication, commitment, enjoyment, purpose, trust.

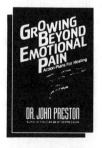

GROWING BEYOND EMOTIONAL PAIN: Action Plans for Healing
John Preston, Psy.D.
Softcover: $12.95   1993   288 pp
Solid, no fads help in overcoming emotional pain. Experienced psychologist offers guidance for making it through difficult times.

GUERRILLA KINDNESS: A Manual of Good Works, Kind Acts and Thoughtful Deeds
Gavin Whitsett
Softcover: $8.95   1993   160pp
An action manual filled with hundreds of everyday kindnesses and thoughtful ways to brighten the world.

Impact Publishers®
POST OFFICE BOX 1094
SAN LUIS OBISPO, CALIFORNIA 93406

Please see the following page for more books.

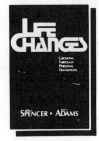
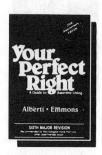